T0042070

ALSO BY KEN REID

Hockey Card Stories: True Tales from Your Favourite Players

One Night Only: Conversations with the NHL's One-Game Wonders

Hockey Card Stories 2: 59 More True Tales from Your Favourite Players

Eddie Shack: Hockey's Most Entertaining Stories (with Ken Reid)

One to Remember: Stories from 39 Members of the NHL's One Goal Club

Dennis Maruk: The Unforgettable Story of Hockey's Forgotten 60-Goal Man (with Dennis Maruk)

KEN REID'S
HOMETOWN
HOCKEY
HEROES

KEN REID

Published by Simon & Schuster

NEW YORK   LONDON   TORONTO

SYDNEY   NEW DELHI

SIMON &
SCHUSTER
CANADA

Simon & Schuster Canada
A Division of Simon & Schuster, LLC
166 King Street East, Suite 300
Toronto, Ontario M5A 1J3

Copyright © 2023 by Ken Reid

All rights reserved, including the right to reproduce this book or portions thereof in any form whatsoever. For information, address Simon & Schuster Canada Subsidiary Rights Department, 166 King Street East, Suite 300, Toronto, Ontario, M5A 1J3.

This Simon & Schuster Canada edition October 2023

SIMON & SCHUSTER CANADA and colophon are trademarks
of Simon & Schuster, LLC

For information about special discounts for bulk purchases, please contact Simon & Schuster Special Sales at 1-800-268-3216 or CustomerService@simonandschuster.ca.

Manufactured in the United States of America

3   5   7   9   10   8   6   4   2

Library and Archives Canada Cataloguing in Publication
Title: Ken Reid's hometown hockey heroes / Ken Reid.
Other titles: Hometown hockey heroes
Names: Reid, Ken, 1974- author.
Description: Simon & Schuster Canada edition.
Identifiers: Canadiana (print) 20230218024 | Canadiana (ebook) 20230218032 |
ISBN 9781668015018 (softcover) | ISBN 9781668015032 (EPUB)
Subjects: LCSH: Hockey—Canada—Anecdotes. | LCSH: Hockey—Social aspects—
Canada—Anecdotes. | LCSH: Hockey—Canada. | LCSH: Hockey—Social aspects—Canada.
Classification: LCC GV848.4.C3 R45 2023 | DDC 796.9620971—dc23

Image Credits: 15: Courtesy of the author; 32: Courtesy of Robbie Forbes; 49: Courtesy of Bruce Campbell; 69: Courtesy of Alex Gallant/Summerside B&G; 82: Courtesy of New Brunswick Sports Hall of Fame; 96: Courtesy of Keven Cloutier; 107: Courtesy of Erin McGonigal; 119: Courtesy of Kevin Tucker; 133: Courtesy of Paul Polillo; 145: Courtesy of therinklive.com; 165: Courtesy of Cliff Duchesne; 183: Courtesy of Tyson Wuttunee; 197: Courtesy of Randy Keller; 214: Courtesy of Zane Jakubec; 226: Courtesy of the McTeer family; 238: Courtesy of Ruth Woodacre

ISBN 978-1-6680-1501-8
ISBN 978-1-6680-1503-2 (ebook)

*To all small-town hockey heroes, who passed
the love of the game on to the next generation*

Contents

CONTENTS

Dana "T-Pot" Johnston

Pictou, Nova Scotia

I grew up in Pictou, a small town on the Northumberland Shore of Nova Scotia, population around 5,000. It's a beautiful little harbour town. The entire town is basically a hill up from the glistening water. Some of the oldest buildings are built from stone brought all the way over from Scotland. In fact, the first Scottish settlers to arrive in Nova Scotia arrived in my hometown on the ship *Hector* in 1773. The only thing that marred the town's beauty was the pulp mill across the harbour. That monstrosity of concrete and stacks filled the air with what ten-year-old me figured was just smoke. I'm still not sure exactly what it was, but I do know one thing: it stunk. When it rained, whatever got belched out of the mill floated across the harbour and made the town smell like a giant rotten egg. Funny thing was, after a while you didn't notice it anymore. People from outside of town sure did, but it's like anything you grow up with: it becomes normal.

We kids didn't let that stench ruin our days because Pictou was the perfect spot to grow up. All the kids in town went to the same schools, in the same order: Dawson, followed by Patterson, then McCulloch Junior High, and finally Pictou Academy. The people of Pictou were particularly proud of our high school. It was the first nondenominational school in the province, and it gave out top-notch scholarships. (I hated the place, but let's save that story for another book.)

Our town was about as Nova Scotia as you could get. Beaches were everywhere. I hated sand, so the beach was not for me. I was more into baseball and golf in the summer. We had a massive 1,800-yard, par-32 golf course that overlooked the harbour. The golf course was a beautiful sight, as long as you ignored the pulp mill in full view or avoided catching a glimpse of a certain former provincial court judge swimming in the number 6 water hole in some state of undress, looking for golf balls in the tiny harbour inlet. And if the thought of hitting a straight shot across the water was not intimidating enough for a ten- or eleven-year-old, you also had to make sure you didn't duff the ball, sending it over a cliff and into the water below, where said former judge would be swimming in the salt water in his tighty-whities, or maybe less.

During summer, kids divided their time between the golf course and baseball fields, the soccer fields and tennis courts; but when winter rolled in, our golf clubs, gloves, racquets, and balls were put away and our focus turned to hockey, and hockey alone.

Like a lot of hockey-loving kids who grew up in the eighties (and for decades before), Saturday night meant *Hockey Night in Canada* on CBC. In Pictou, the game would come on at 9:00 pm, and in my much younger days that meant a sleepover for my little brother and me at our grandparents' house. Who knows what Mom and Dad were up to those nights, but for Peter and me it meant Nana's famous egg salad sandwiches and the *Hockey Night in Canada* broadcast.

One of my most vivid memories was a penalty shot Wayne

Gretzky took on goalie Michel "Bunny" Larocque. I pretty much guaranteed to my papa that Wayne was going to score. And why wouldn't he? This was the 1981–82 season: Wayne was on his way to a record 92 goals. The Great One skated in and eventually darted to his left. Larocque stood tall in his old brown pads and sweet duckbill mask with "Bunny" emblazoned on the front. He kept the pads together and made the save. I have no idea who won that game—I assume the Oilers, as they were playing the Leafs in 1982, after all—but that save still lingers in my mind.

A few months later, in summer, my family moved from the outskirts of town to Patterson Street and my life and my hockey nights in Canada changed for good. We lived right next to Westwood Drive, a neighbourhood right out of *The Wonder Years*: kids and young families everywhere. We lived right up the hill from the Hector Arena. As soon as the ice froze in the rink, I pretty much lived at the place. There was after-school skating on Monday, Wednesday, and Friday, plus Friday-night skating and minor hockey all day Saturday. I soon discovered that the Pictou Mariners' Junior C team played every Saturday evening at 7:30 pm sharp. I had never seen anything like the Mariners, except on television. The players wore crisp blue-and-white sweaters, each with a cool-looking anchor on the front. They even wore matching blue-and-white socks that fit perfectly with their blue-and-white sweaters. The team took a full warm-up, and the players looked like men. Some of them had moustaches, some of them had long hair, and some of them even smoked. (Actually, a lot of them smoked.) These were grown men, hockey players right down the hill from me. In my ten-year-old mind, there was no difference between these guys and the players I watched on *Hockey Night in Canada*.

Soon enough a new Saturday hockey night tradition began. I'd gather up my little brother, meet up with my buddies David and Mark on the way, and we'd all make the trek down the hill to the Hector Arena. We'd arrive at 7:00 pm, pay our dollar to get in, buy a pack or two of hockey cards, and then go stand right above the penalty box. No parental accompaniment required—the only rule from Mom and Dad was, "Don't go down to the far end by the tractor." (We didn't have a Zamboni; we had a tractor.) The far end of the rink was usually shrouded in a cloud of smoke, and sometimes it smelled different than the Player's Lights my grandfather inhaled. When things got rowdy, a bottle might fly through the air and land on the ice. It usually wasn't a pop bottle. Sometimes the bottles were clear, or perhaps larger ones decorated with a sailor on the front, or brown ones, like the kind Dad drank from on Saturday afternoons. Regardless, they never had a problem finding the ice. There was no Plexiglas around the rink, just a chicken wire barrier at each end. Sitting by the boards meant risking your life. Every second game or so a kid would take a stick or puck in the face and a familiar announcement followed: "If Dr. Dan Reid is in the building, could he please make his way to the arena office."

Dr. Reid, my dad, fixed up a lot of faces.

When the Mariners headed out for warm-up, we'd turn around, make a quick trek down the stairs right behind us, and pat each player on the shoulder as he took to the ice. The names still stand out in my mind: Hebert, Turner, Dort, MacDonald, Heighton, Murphy. Soon, one name emerged that in my mind stood above all the rest: Johnston. Dana Johnston.

They called him "T-Pot"—maybe because he was short and stout. He'd also become known as simply "T" and "The Sweet

One." T-Pot and the Mariners became part of my Saturday-night double-header ritual. I'd watch the Mariners and then race home around 10:00 pm to watch the rest of *Hockey Night in Canada*. I'd catch the final two periods of the Oilers or Canadiens on television, but I'd always catch the full three periods of T-Pot in person.

To me there was no bigger star in the game than T. He was right there on my Mount Rushmore of hockey with Wayne, Guy, and whomever else you want to throw in as the fourth guy. T was my original hockey hero, and it turns out I was not alone. The entire town loved the Sweet One. They still do. T-Pot was the original hometown legend and, in my mind, the legendary Hector Arena became "The House That T Built."

Saturday after Saturday I'd watch T do his thing. He stood about 5'8", could grow a moustache or beard in a sprint—you'd never know what kind of facial hair he'd have on any given night—and could seemingly score at will. He had the hardest snapshot I'd ever seen, always bar down. He wore number 8, and so every kid in town wore number 8. (Years later, my buddy Rob was out for a game of shinny with T, who looked around and asked, offhandedly, "Why is everyone wearing eight?" Rob had a simple answer for him: "You!")

T had that one thing that would thrill any hockey fan of any age. T had a flair for the dramatic. As I mentioned before, if you needed a big goal, T was always there. "It was just being in the right spot in the right time," he tells me. "You gotta put the puck where the goalie is . . . not where he is going to be. A lot of times I'd shoot it right at him. He'd think that I'd be going somewhere else, and he'd move out of the way. Five-hole was always my best. I'd make the slightest little move to get the goalie to open the legs, and well, you got a freebie."

It wasn't just that T scored a lot of goals. It was how he scored them. If the Mariners were ever in a pinch, T would always come through with a big goal. Overtime in the League finals against the Thorburn Mohawks? No problem. Just cue T. He'd always come through, and we all loved him for it.

When the Mariners went on the road midweek to what we called the upper towns—places across the harbour like Stellarton or Trenton—I'd rush into my parents' room for John "Brother" MacDonald's sports news at ten to eight on CKEC radio the next morning. More often than not, MacDonald would announce that T had scored two goals in the Mariners' latest win.

In spring 1983, the Mariners advanced all the way to the Nova Scotia finals and for the first two games of their provincial finals series they had to make the long trek to North Sydney, roughly 250 kilometres from Pictou. I have no idea how we did it, but my brother and I managed to convince my parents to take us to North Sydney to watch a bunch of local teenagers play hockey. My parents obviously knew that there were no future NHLers on the team, but perhaps they saw the dreams in my eyes, and the potential heartache if I didn't get to see T do his thing.

My parents piled into the car with me, Peter, my sister, Katie, and my buddy Dave, and we made the three-plus-hour drive to North Sydney. As soon as game one started it was obvious that T and the powerful Mariners would be in no danger of falling to the young, feather-haired teenagers from industrial Cape Breton. The rout was on: soon enough, with the Mariners nursing a healthy lead, T was alone in the slot. He wound up for a massive slapshot, raising his wooden Sherwood over his head, and unleashed—except this time he fanned on the puck. Still, the North Sydney goalie was no match: watching the Sweet One's windup, he stood up as straight as he could, no doubt terrified of the certain heat to follow. Coming off that rare T miss, the puck slowly curled its way toward the goal line, with no sweeping required, and it just . . . crossed the line. If memory serves me, the goalie had closed his eyes in fear. T had scored again, this time on a phantom slapshot, and to this day I swear he did it on purpose.

The Mariners took both games in North Sydney, returned home, and then took two more to complete the sweep. After the game four win, Hector Arena was a madhouse, the two thousand or so fans jammed into the rink going wild. The smoke picked up, the cheering picked up, there were hugs everywhere, and suddenly there was a stampede to the spot where my buddies Dave and Mark, my little brother, Peter, and I had been camped out all season long. Kids arrived en masse, and they were all looking for the same thing: sticks. It was on—the fight for a Mariners stick. Of course, there was only one stick that I wanted, but alas, I and my tiny buddies were cast aside by massive twelve-to-fourteen-year-olds. Not only did I leave that night without T's stick . . . I didn't get a stick at all. And I was so close to getting the stick that belonged to my hometown hockey hero.

My brother and I were practically in tears. We moped around the house all day Sunday. How could we, the Mariners' biggest fans—T's biggest fans!—who had been there all year long, who had followed the Mariners all the way up to Cape Breton, leave championship night stickless?

On Monday the talk at school was, of course, all about the Mariners. Everyone knew someone who had snagged a stick. It was a horrible week. Not only would I not see T—well on his way to local legendary status—play for another six months, I didn't have a stick, either.

Luckily there is nothing my mom would not do for me, including contacting T's mother and making a trek to T's house. The Johnston residence sat, appropriately enough, on 88 Front Street, or as the locals knew it, the top of Battery Hill. It was a beautiful old house that overlooked the harbour. By Wednesday of that week my mom had heard enough. I guess she made a call to Mrs. Johnston.

When we arrived home from school that day, Mom said she had something for each of us. We followed her into the living room and there they were: two authentic Dana Johnston game-used hockey sticks. You could have given me a Wayne Gretzky Titan and I would not have been half as happy as I was that day. Sure, I was a righty and T was a lefty, but this was my T-Pot stick. I held it, and then I saw the writing, halfway up the shaft: "To Kenny, Hope to see you next year, Dana Johnston, #8." It was a goddamn beautiful thing, and it was mine.

That summer, I went from pretending I was Guy Lafleur while playing road hockey to imagining I was T-Pot. We all taped our sticks like T as well—with white and black tape. He was my hometown hockey hero, and as the years went by, he became the hero of the whole friggin' town. Starting that year, 1983, the Mariners went on a streak of four straight Nova Scotia Junior C titles.

It seemed there was nothing T couldn't do. As I mentioned earlier, my post-hockey-season summers were all about baseball and golf. My buddy Mark and I discovered, after that hockey season was over, that T was our very own Bo Jackson, long before Jackson became famous. There was no better third baseman in town than T, who played for Caribou in the local fastball league. Today most people call it softball. We called it "whip pitch." Now that I lived in a neighbourhood in the middle of town, summers were an adventure. We'd take our bikes everywhere, including down to CN Field on the harbour to watch T play third. He was fearless. If he thought a bunt was coming, he'd set up shop about five feet from home. If he didn't, he'd hug the line down at third. Soon enough, all the kids, including me, would imitate how T played at third. If we snatched a grounder, we'd do exactly what T would do: make the grab, take a look at the ball, and then make an over-the-top throw to first that always one-hopped into the first baseman's glove to get the runner just in time. That's how T did it, so that's how we did it. Years later, a rumour circulated that T turned down a chance to play for the national softball team when he was only sixteen. I wouldn't doubt it.

Then there was T-Pot on the golf course, where he would always win the championship. The par-32 Pictou Golf and Country Club was no golfer's paradise, but it was our beloved slice of the game. The place was not irrigated, and the ground was hard as a rock, so T naturally played the bump-and-run to perfection. It was almost like he was playing pool on the course, which I guess explains why he was also the best pool player in town. He would win game after game at the tavern, or so we were told by the kids who were old enough to get into the Tav. When I was old enough, I found out the legend was true. Yes, T-Pot was the Tav pool champion and from the pictures I saw on the wall he was also the darts champion.

One Saturday afternoon, many years later, while I was sitting at the Tav having a few with my buddies, I found out that T was also the Pictou Lobster Carnival lobster-banding champion. What's lobster banding, you ask? When a fisherman takes a lobster out of a trap, he puts elastic bands over its claws, so the lobsters won't fight each other when they're clustered together in the holding tank. Two claws, two bands. At the carnival every July, a dozen lobsters were set out in front of the banding contestants, and the fastest fishermen in town would show up to compete for the title of fastest bander. Of course it's T—if it is a competition, the man wins it. It just so happened, that particular Saturday afternoon, while I was at the Tav with my buddies, in walked T-Pot. He came through the door holding a knife above his head. It was the first-place prize from Pictou's famous knife maker, Grohmann Knives, for winning yet another lobster-banding championship. By this point in my life, T was an absolute legend.

After that first season in the eighties of watching T and the Mariners, the next three seasons were full of moments that build up the legend. As one might imagine, Junior C hockey in rural Nova Scotia had its fair share of fights, even brawls. T handled conflict differently: he would rarely drop the gloves. All he needed to settle an opponent down was his legendary headlock. T had massive forearms, like a real-life Popeye; they were responsible for his cannon of a shot, after all. If things got out of hand on the ice, T would simply apply a headlock that would make Hulk Hogan proud.

Year after year, T and the Mariners would meet the dreaded Thorburn Mohawks in the county finals. Thorburn was just a little tiny community about twenty minutes away. But to me it was a hockey hotbed. It was the home of Lowell MacDonald, who had played in the NHL. And the Mohawks got to pick their team from the vast rural area of eastern Pictou County. They were a dreaded team. Fifteen hundred fans might pack Hector Arena for our home games, but things were different when it came to

Thorburn's small rink—that tiny barn couldn't even hold three hundred. No problem. The solution was to hold the Mohawks' home games in massive New Glasgow Stadium, which could fit 2,500, maybe 3,000 fans. A twenty-minute drive from Pictou and a perfect setting for T to add to his legendary status.

It was the 1984 finals. Mark and I were camped down in the first row of the stadium, and there must have been three hundred people packed in there. We had our homemade signs. I think mine said "Go Mariners," but Mark's sign was perfect: a drawing of a T-Pot with a hockey stick. It was obvious who Mark's hero was—the same as mine.

With two seconds to go in the game and the Mariners down by one, Bruce Hebert scored to tie up the game. Mark and I went ballistic, jumping and screaming. We both started frantically kicking the boards, and I'm not sure if it was Mark or me, but we repeatedly—and unintentionally—kicked a lady's purse into the boards. (Luckily the owner was a good sport and just laughed it off.) We had two seconds and then a fifteen-minute flood of the rink to catch our breath and then it was off to overtime, which netted nothing, and with the score still tied, off we went to double overtime.

Now I could describe what happened in double overtime—but I think I'll hand it over to the man himself. In a *New Glasgow Evening News* article from 2013, written shortly before those Mariners teams of the 1980s were inducted into the Pictou County Sports Hall of Fame, T described how it went down: "Tim MacDonald, Shawn MacDonald, and I went in on a three-on-two. They split the defence and left me wide open to beat their goalie short side. I'll never forget it." It was another unforgettable championship year for T and the Mariners, the second of four in a row.

The highlight of the following season had nothing to with anything T-Pot did on the ice. During the playoffs, I caught a ride out to a game in the upper towns with Mark and his family. His dad, Millard, a Mariners executive, said he'd drop by the rink just in case anyone missed a ride. And there stood T; he'd missed a team ride heading to the game. He jumped in the backseat and sat right between Mark and me. For us, that twenty-minute ride to the game was a like a twenty-minute audience with the pope. Imagine being a kid and getting to share a car ride with your hockey hero. I got to do that.

The legendary status that T formed in my mind, and in the minds of an entire town, is as fresh now as it was when I was a kid. Years later, too, the legend is still going strong. I remember Pictou mayor Joe Hawes once saying to me, "How come T-Pot isn't in the Pictou County Sports Hall of Fame as an individual athlete? He's the only guy I know who won the Junior C championship, Westville Town League championship, the Nova League championship, and the Pictou Town League championship." Wherever T went, he won. (The rumour was he played in Westville because he got free dental work.)

The legend of the Sweet One shines brightly on Pictou every Boxing Day as well. For my buddies back home, Boxing Day is just as special, and as spiritual, as Christmas Day, because that's when the T-Pot Cup takes place. My friend Craig Clarke organizes it. About fifty guys show up at Hector Arena at 9:00 am on Boxing Day, consume some stuff, divide into four teams, and play for the T-Pot Cup. I even got to play in it one year. T, of course, is the main attraction. He does not say much and tends to do his talking with his stick, always scoring at will on my buddy Scott and any other goalie who might be in his way. He presents the winning team with the T-Pot Cup—a teapot Craig screwed on to the top of an old trophy. More often than not, T has to present the cup to his own team, because T simply wins.

Then there are the "T" shirts—yes, T-shirts. One year when I arrived home in Pictou for the Lobster Carnival, before we headed to the beer garden, Craig presented me with my very own limited-edition "T" shirt, designed and made up by T's old Junior C teammate Robbie Marks. On the front is a picture of T on the stern of a lobster boat with a five-pound lobster in each hand and a cigarette in his mouth. Above T is printed, simply: "The Legend." No further explanation needed. The highlight of the carnival that year was running into T while wearing the "T" shirt and getting a picture with my old hero. Robbie only printed twenty of those shirts; he could have printed off 888 and they would have sold out. They were the talk of the carnie.

My cohost on *Sportsnet Central*, Evanka Osmak, came to the carnival one year. All she wanted was everyone's favourite T-Pot story and she was regaled with them—story after story. After hearing about game-winning goals, golf shots, home runs, and more, her favourite came from T's old buddy Randy Mansour. He told her no kid in town made a better snow fort than T. My hockey hero could do it all.

Sometimes the world comes full circle. One time, when I was working at TSN, the network went to Pictou for *SportsCentre*. (A live *SportsCentre* from my seaside hometown, imagine!) The anchors, Dutchy and Jenn, ran into T-Pot—it's a given that if you're going to Pictou, you're likely going to run into T. He set up shop on the remake of the legendary ship *Hector*—the vessel that brought the first Scottish settlers to Nova Scotia—and showed them how to band lobsters. Child's play for T but a bit of a challenge for Dutchy and Jenn, who nailed it nonetheless. T did this while wearing a homemade shirt that proclaimed, "I heart Ken Reid." I heart you, too, T!

It's funny what sticks with you through the years. When I was eight years old, I saw a guy who I thought was the greatest hockey player I've ever seen. Over the years, I've covered the NHL, interviewed Hall of Famers, and witnessed their on-ice exploits, but for me, the guy I saw when I was eight is still sitting tall on my hockey pedestal, right up there with Gretzky and Lafleur. Dana Johnston was one of my first hockey heroes; the first hockey hero I could see in person, someone who I could run into at the rink in the morning and then see play that night.

T gave me the gift of seeing my real-life hockey legend up close. How many kids could just walk around town and "spot" Wayne Gretzky or Mike Bossy? We could spot T on any given day. Maybe he'd be walking down the street—we'd scream, "Hey, T!" and he'd always give us a hearty "Hey, boys!" and a wave back. But man, we were too shy to go up to him and say anything else.

Dana Johnston is my hometown legend, and this country is full of guys like T-Pot. Not everyone grew up in the big city. Not everyone could take a streetcar to Maple Leaf Gardens or the Metro to the Montreal Forum. For thousands, if not millions of us, our hockey legends were the local high school kids, fishermen, millworkers, or farmers who suited up right before our eyes, taking on the hockey legends of that "other" town.

I could go on and on about the Sweet One, and trust me, I have. Over the years I have moved from Nova Scotia to Calgary, to Ottawa, to Edmonton, and finally to Toronto, and at every stop I've turned coworkers into fans of T. Maybe they are fans because he's relatable. He's the star we always wanted to be. Who wouldn't want to be their hometown hero? Or maybe they are fans of T because they had a hometown legend just like him.

T-Pot and I at the Pictou Lobster Carnival.

CHAPTER 1

Robbie Forbes

Corner Brook, Newfoundland, and Halifax, Nova Scotia

The produce section? That used to be the penalty box. Over there by the chips and pop, maybe that's where a massive body check was thrown. In the corner, that's where Section A was, which housed the wildest fans in town.

"They were the craziest people who grew up in Corner Brook," says retired schoolteacher George Dolomount. "One night they brought a chocolate cake to the rink and threw it at Stephenville defenceman Kevin Morrison."

You can buy a cake in this building now: it's the Colemans Food Centre in Corner Brook, Newfoundland. Years ago, it fed the community with the finest hockey around when it was Humber Gardens, home of the 1986 Allan Cup champion Corner Brook Royals. "I tell my son [when we get groceries], Nick, who is twenty-three, all the stories," says George. "I say, 'This was the hockey rink. When you come in this front door, this is where you came into the ticket booth in the Humber Gardens.'"

In the mid-1980s, every man, woman, and child in Corner Brook wanted a seat in Humber Gardens. Corner Brook was a pulp and paper town. Its mill was built in the early 1920s, smack in the middle of town, at the edge of the Humber River, which eventually opens and flows into the Gulf of St. Lawrence on the west coast of Newfoundland. For years, the people of Corner Brook harvested the forests of the surrounding area, turning wood into newsprint. "The paper industry was still going very well in the seventies and eighties," says George. So were the Royals.

George was a university student in the mid-1980s, studying education. He'd go on to teach phys ed and health classes. This was useful training since Humber Gardens gave him a firsthand look at the dangers of secondhand smoke. "I'd tell my students, 'In the hockey rink you could barely see the players by the third period. All you could see was the blue smoke from cigarettes.' My students didn't believe me, but it was true."

In spring 1985, the Corner Brook Royals, of the Newfoundland Senior Hockey League, took the town of thirty thousand on a ride they had never been on before. The team won the Herder, the Newfoundland hockey championship, but that was not enough. The Royals were in search of a national title. They wanted an Allan Cup championship, and the town wanted it, too.

It seemed like destiny. Corner Brook hosted the national quarterfinals and the Royals won that series. Then they hosted a national semifinal series. They won that, too. There was only one more series to host: the Allan Cup Finals.

The Thunder Bay Twins represented western Canada. Corner Brook represented the east. It was a best-of-seven series, with all seven games, if necessary, to be played in the cozy confines of Humber Gardens. By "cozy" I mean a little barn with rock-hard boards and rock-hard ice, which made for a fast, physical game.

The Royals had their challenge in front of them with the Twins, the defending Allan Cup champions. The people of

Corner Brook had a challenge as well—good luck getting a ticket. The Gardens held three thousand, officially, and everyone wanted a seat: "Trying to get a ticket was next to impossible," says George. His girlfriend at the time (now wife) did what a lot of other kids did to secure playoff tickets: she snuck out of the house to grab a spot in line: "They'd have a fire barrel in the line [to keep warm]. Everyone would be around the fire barrel lining up for the tickets. They'd get their tickets, get home, and wake up and go to school. It was big to get a ticket to the Royals games."

The first three games of the best-of-seven series went exactly according to plan for the three-thousand-plus fans that jammed into the Gardens. The Royals won all three games. Winning the Allan Cup was a mere formality at this point. Then came game four: "People were hanging from the rafters. You'd've had to see it to believe me," says George. "They were going to win the Allan Cup. The next thing you know, they were playing the game and Tony White wasn't there."

Tony White was the player-coach of the Royals. He had been one of the team's top players that season. The Newfoundlander was one of the biggest draws at the Gardens, not surprisingly, considering he once scored 25 goals in a single NHL season. Rumours swirled around town as to why White was not there. (Years later, a 2018 newspaper story said he was unavailable because he had been accepted into the Vancouver Fire Department.) The Royals didn't win another game in the series. Thunder Bay did the impossible and erased a 3–0 series deficit. They won game seven in Corner Brook by the slimmest of margins, a 5–4 win.

The Royals had it in the bag. All they needed was one more win. But they could not do it, and the town was crushed. "The night they lost, it was heart-wrenching," says George, almost forty years later. "They were playing all the games from the quarter-finals to semifinals and finals, they were all played in Humber Gardens. The community was just abuzz. And then to lose those last four games, it was, it was . . ." His voice trails off. George still can't put it into words.

About that same time, a ferry ride and one very long drive away, a young kid from Halifax was giving the fans in Fredericton, New Brunswick, a season they had never seen before. Robbie Forbes was an undersized, highly skilled forward who scored everywhere he went. He started his Junior career in PEI for the Junior A Charlottetown Eagles. He tied for the league lead in scoring and was chosen Rookie of the Year and Most Valuable Player.

That season was enough to earn him a shot with the Laval Voisins of the Quebec Major Junior Hockey League. It was a big step up. Forbes scored 17 points in 19 games—not too bad. The team had another decent centre, a sixteen-year-old named Mario Lemieux, who, in 64 games, put up 96 points to lead the team. (Robbie's and Mario's paths would cross again years later.) Forbes wrapped up his Junior career with his hometown Halifax Lions. In his final year of Junior, he set a Metro Valley Junior Hockey League record with 130 points in 40 games. "I was recruited by a number of universities across Canada," says Forbes.

He chose the University of New Brunswick. Then called the Red Devils, the program had a strong tradition. Forbes moved to the New Brunswick capital and didn't miss a beat. He centered a line with an old Halifax teammate, Mark Jeffrey, on one side and future pro John LeBlanc on the other. The trio finished first, fourth, and fifth in league scoring. They combined for 180 points. Forbes led the way with 30 goals and 34 assists for 64 points in just 24 games. They are rookie records that still stand for a program that has won nine Canadian titles. It was a great season for Forbes and his linemates, but not for the team: "UNB had gone to the national championship the previous year. We added a few more bodies but we lost some as well. So that season we didn't do as well as we should have."

UNB had high hopes for that 1984–85 season but they only finished sixth in their conference; that was it for Robbie Forbes as a Red Devil. After one year in Fredericton, he decided to go pro.

He had a sniff from the St. Louis Blues but didn't attend their main camp. Back in his hometown of Halifax he tried out for the Nova Scotia Oilers. They were the top farm team of the defending Stanley Cup champs. The organization was deep in offensive talent, and they didn't have a spot for the hometown kid in Halifax. There was an opportunity with Peoria in the now defunct International Hockey League (IHL), but something else popped up on Forbes's radar. Halifax was about as far east as you could get, but not quite: "My friend Stan Hennigar was playing in Corner Brook, and they had gone to the Allan Cup Finals. They said they were one or two guys away from winning the national championship. Stan said he could have the guys from Corner Brook call me and I said, 'Sure.' I spoke to the guys in Corner Brook. I spoke to the guys in Peoria [Illinois]. I said, 'Screw it. I'm going to play a season in Newfoundland.'"

Robbie Forbes was twenty-two years old. He had no idea he was about to become an icon in Corner Brook and across Newfoundland.

"Robbie Forbes is one of the greatest imports to ever play in the Newfoundland Senior Hockey League and that is fine company. He was a hero of mine." That's a quote from former NHLer

Terry Ryan. Kids from Newfoundland don't often play in the NHL, let alone get chosen in the first round. But on July 8, 1995, that dream came true for Ryan and his family.

A few years earlier, Terry's dad, Terry Sr., who had played pro in the 1970s, moved with Terry Jr. all the way across Canada in pursuit of the NHL dream. Terry Jr. had dominated the Peewee ranks of Newfoundland, so they moved to British Columbia while mother Gail stayed at home. Fourteen-year-old Terry went straight from Peewee hockey in Newfoundland to playing with men in the Rocky Mountain Junior A Hockey League. A few years later he was a WHL superstar for the Tri-City Americans.

At the 1995 draft in Edmonton, Terry's favourite childhood team, the Montreal Canadiens, took him with the eighth overall pick in the NHL Draft. It was the highest a Newfoundlander had ever been selected. This was a kid who grew up on the Rock, dreaming of life in the NHL. His heroes were Gretzky and Lemieux, and another guy as well. He was a guy the rest of the kids in attendance at the draft never saw on Saturday-night TV. "Robbie Forbes, for me, was just larger than life," says Terry. "That's really the way to put it. At the time my favourite NHL team was the Montreal Canadiens. They won the Stanley Cup in 1986, and I kid you not, if you had said to me, 'Do you want to meet Rob Forbes or do you want to meet Bob Gainey?' I would take Rob Forbes. And Bob Gainey was the captain of my favourite NHL team," says the former NHLer.

Fandom like that is earned. In late September 1985, Robbie Forbes headed for Newfoundland. He made the trip through the Nova Scotia highways, all the way from his hometown of Halifax, into Cape Breton, where he finally came to a stop in North Sydney. Forbes caught the ferry and made the 178-kilometre journey across the Cabot Strait to Port aux Basques, Newfoundland. From there it was a 200-plus-kilometre drive to the unknown, a little town called Corner Brook. He loved it: "Corner Brook was a place where I immediately felt at home. I don't know what it was. I guess just the people and the culture. Everything really resonated with me."

It's hard not to fall in love with Newfoundland. Forbes did what many first-time visitors to the Rock do: he got "screeched" in right away. Getting screeched in goes like this: Many a Newfoundlander will conduct a ceremony for first-time visitors to the Island. The locals put a "come from away" through a short ceremony that consists of invoking a few Island phrases, a shot of local Screech rum, and then a kiss on a codfish. Voila! You are screeched in. (If you've ever heard the phrase *kiss the cod*, this is what I'm talking about.)

Then it was time to get down to business. Forbes knew the mission. "The nucleus was basically there from the team that went to the Allan Cup the year before. It was a pretty good club. Everyone just kind of got to work. There was only one goal: a national championship."

Forbes was an import. In other words, he was a non-Newfoundlander. Imports were paid well for their services, and they were expected to deliver. The league was full of high-priced, high-talent imports: guys who had played in the minors and even in the NHL. Now Forbes was one of them. "I knew there were going to be expectations to do what I do, which is score goals and put up points. I knew that going in. And I knew that based on the roster from the previous year, the Royals were going to be really competitive."

So the journey began. Forbes looked the part of the sniper,

too. He had that cool, hunched-over skating style and rocked the standard moustache of the day. He wore nothing more than a Gretzky JOFA on his head, but his stick wasn't a Gretzky Titan. "To be honest, I used whatever stick was on sale at the time. I'd use whatever the trainer would buy."

Forbes soon discovered that as friendly as Newfoundlanders were around town, it was a different story once the games began. The first game he played was in Stephenville, about an hour away, against Corner Brook's biggest rival, the aptly named Jets. They played in an old rink that used to be an air hangar. "We went into Stephenville, and they had a big, tough team. They had Kevin Morrison [a former WHA all-star who once had 348 penalty minutes in the old tough-as-nails Eastern League] and Gordie Gallant [aka "Machine Gun," who twice led the WHA in penalty minutes]. And we had a tough team, too. We had Stan and Danny Cormier and a guy by the name of Stevie Gallant [no relation to Gordie] from Prince Edward Island." In 1982–83, Cormier was third in the QMJHL in PIMs, no small feat in the Q, then or now. With lineups like this, fights were bound to happen. "The first one was usually at fifteen minutes of the first period."

A full-scale line brawl broke out in Stephenville. Welcome to Newfoundland, Robbie Forbes! Fists were flying. Fans were screaming. The kid in the JOFA found a guy and held on: "I forget who I paired up with, but it would have been mostly to watch. There were some big-time tilts going on all over the ice and I thought to myself, 'This can't be how it's going to go the whole year.' But it was chippy the first few games. We settled in over the season and ended up having a really great rivalry. We were two really good teams. Those Senior teams in Stephenville and Corner Brook were two of the best Senior teams in the country."

about my Atom hockey team, and I told him all about it. I told him I had just been named captain of the team. He seemed interested and looking back now, and knowing because I've been in that position, he was probably just humouring me. But he was really good at it. He just seemed to me like the Steve Yzerman of the league back then."

Forbes was making a name for himself on the Rock with his skill, but also his toughness. Not fighting, but the toughness it takes to go to the front of the net, to battle, to take the abuse. Forbes led the Newfoundland league that year with 117 points, 21 more than the runner-up. To do that in this league, you had to go to the dirty areas, like the front of the net, an area that was protected by big, burly defencemen like Kevin Morrison, the former NHLer.

"For me I always got to the net. You try to time it so that Kevin wasn't there—get behind him. Kevin took that space very personally. For me, when you're playing against Kevin or anyone else, it's just getting to the net. Always within that kind of ten-foot area is where you scored goals. So that was always my objective," Robbie says. "There's always fear with guys like Kevin on the ice, because they're really big and tough guys out there. Fair guys, too. He's going to play the game hard. But it's either go to the net or not. But if you don't go to the net, you're not going to score goals. That still stands today. You got to go to the net to get goals."

So that's what Forbes did, game after game, on the road or at the old Humber Gardens. "Those boards weren't very forgiving at Humber. It was an amazing place. You'd come out for our home games, and it would be dark and smoky. The fans would be crazy. There was no forgiveness. It was a very small rink. The ice was so fast and hard. Small arenas are really good, too, because there's not as much territory to take for you to get to the net. That arena was always, always rocking. The place was small, and it was just conducive to really fast and hard hockey."

All through 1985–86, Forbes went to the net and scored goals. There were hits all around him. He put up points. There were fights all around him. He put up points. There was bedlam in Section A: "I remember one night they threw a suitcase at either Morrison or one of the Jets. In other words, 'Pack up and go home, you're no good,'" says George.

Forbes kept scoring. But like a lot of the guys I talked to about this, there is a total absence of ego about those points. "I don't have a memory of any specific goal. It's funny. I don't know if it's my brain not having enough space in there. I don't remember a lot of the individual stuff. I don't remember goals or assists. I just remember playing and winning."

That and the boys, his teammates, the room. "We had an amazing room in Corner Brook, incredible guys. It was a different era. We had guys having a dart [a cigarette] and a Coke in between periods. The other thing about Corner Brook was that we had some really great imports, but we also had an incredible group of local guys as well. That's part of the alchemy. We were a mix of guys—some of us were getting paid, some of us were getting small stipends. There were incredible local guys that kept everything light and positive. They just made the whole thing work."

The whole thing did work. The Royals took out their biggest rival, the Stephenville Jets, in six games to win the Herder. Unlike the previous year, there wouldn't be any lineups around Humber Gardens afterward. There were no home games at all, in fact, as the march to the Allan Cup continued. The Royals were hitting the road. Their first stop after winning the Herder was in

Ontario, where they took on the Flamboro Mott's Clamato's. The team had former NHLers Rocky Saganiuk and Stan Jonathan. The Royals won the series in seven. Then it was on to Nelson, British Columbia. The winner of that series would be crowned 1986 Allan Cup champions. "I remember listening to the games on the radio," says George. "Robbie Forbes was unbelievable. His whole line was. Some people think back to great NHL lines. I think back to the line of Forbes, Cormier, and Stark."

The Royals won the series in four straight games. Mission accomplished. They took the red-eye back to Newfoundland and were greeted by a mad throng at the Stephenville Airport. An eight-kilometre-long motorcade escorted the team back to Humber Gardens. The party was on: "I just felt at home the moment I arrived in Newfoundland. Winning a national championship there was obviously a highlight of my life," says Forbes.

The run to the Allan Cup wasn't cheap: the travel, the hotels, the flights. A media report from 1996, ten years after the championship run, estimated that those two years of challenging for a national title, in 1985 and '86, cost the organization almost one million dollars. As Don Bradshaw, then a sports reporter for the *Western Star* of Corner Brook, said in that CBC report, "I think a lot of people look back on it now and say, 'Well yeah, we lost a lot of money on it, but damn it was worth it.'"

You can tell from listening to George Dolomount that it was. All these years later, he can still go on and on about the Royals and Robbie Forbes. "He was a very admirable player. Everybody loved him. There was nobody that watched Rob Forbes that would criticize anything about him or would say anything bad about him."

That's pretty high praise for a guy who played Senior hockey in Newfoundland in the 1980s. It's the kind of praise an Oilers fan may have for Connor McDavid, a Leafs fan may have for Auston Matthews, or a Penguins fan may have for Sidney Crosby. Especially that last comparison, as hockey runs deep in the Forbes family. In Corner Brook they are always happy to share stories about Robbie Forbes: Sid's uncle, some call him. It's true: years after Forbes tore up the Newfoundland Senior circuit, his nephew Sidney Crosby would become the best player on the planet.

"Yes, he does sound like Sidney," says George. "Absolutely. My son grew up a Sidney Crosby fan. I remember the first time I told him the story of Robbie Forbes, who is Sidney Crosby's uncle, who played with the Royals. He wanted me to tell him more. Everything was Crosby, Crosby, Crosby. He even had a dryer in our front garage, shooting hockey pucks at it. He was that big a Crosby fan. I love Crosby, but there's haters of Crosby out there, jealous people and people who cheer for the other team, and they don't like the Penguins. But there's nothing not to like about Sidney Crosby. And his uncle was exactly the same way. Everybody in Corner Brook loved him. If you talked to anybody in Corner Brook who watched hockey that season, they would tell you that they love Rob Forbes."

It's funny where hockey takes you. It took Robbie Forbes to PEI, then to Laval, Quebec, where he was teammates with his nephew's future teammate (and boss) Mario Lemieux. And yes, they have bumped into each other at one of Robbie's nephew's games since. (I told you they would cross paths again.) "I ran into him at a couple of parties in a couple of events in Pittsburgh. He says he remembers playing with me, but who knows? Mario's a kind guy. I'm sure he's met thousands of people over the years, but I certainly remember it."

Mario was part of Robbie's hockey journey. His nephew Sidney is now part of it, too. So are Robbie's two sons, Robert and William Forbes, who share the goaltending duties for the Junior A South Shore Lumberjacks in Bridgewater, Nova Scotia, not too far from where Robbie now lives.

After the Allan Cup, Forbes spent another year and parts of another season with the Royals before his hockey career took him overseas to Holland, Austria, and England. Forbes was a scorer in Europe as well. During his season in Holland, he scored 127 points, 77 points in 43 games the next year in Austria, and 55 points in 18 games during his final season overseas in England. Then he was back to Nova Scotia to wrap up his competitive hockey career. And yes, in his final season of Senior he led the Bridgewater Blues in scoring.

"For me, that whole journey was just amazing. As you get older, you kind of hold on to all these memories about how you got to where you are, and the journey and the memories that you make. I think that's really important in life for me. I have these buckets of memories from all those towns and have friends that I still stay in touch with from every one of those towns. Corner Brook was one of those places that was really incredibly special."

It was so special that his sons, Robert and William, are often asked by the relatives of their Newfoundland teammates if they are related to *the* Robbie Forbes. "My sons get a kick out of it. They send me texts all the time that they're in Bridgewater, they're in Dartmouth, or they're somewhere and somebody will say, 'Oh, do you know Rob Forbes?' and Robbie will say, 'Yeah, that's my dad.' And they'll tell them a story about watching me play. They really get a kick out of that."

Robbie Forbes will always be a big part of Corner Brook and its hockey history—so much so that his page on eliteprospects.com, the online bible of all things hockey, lists his hometown not as Halifax but as Corner Brook. "My son Robbie says, 'Why don't you change it?' I told him, 'Hey, I really love Halifax, but I really love Corner Brook. And listen, Corner Brook may not be my home, but it always felt like a second home for me, so I'm okay with it.'"

Robbie Forbes (middle) during his playing days with the Corner Brook Royals, flanked by Sheldon Currie (left) and Danny Cormier (right).

CHAPTER 2

Bruce Campbell

New Waterford, Nova Scotia

"I don't know . . . I've never confirmed it," begins Steve MacKenzie, a middle-aged hockey dad who grew up in New Waterford, Nova Scotia. "But you always heard it—the owner of the rink used to pay Bruce extra money to stay out and shoot pucks after warm-up, just so that people would get to the rink early and buy chips and pop and chocolate bars."

"I only did it a couple of times," says Bruce Campbell. "I didn't want to feel I was above the team. I would whistle a few extra slapshots until I hit the crossbar with one or two. Our rink had a low ceiling. If you hit the crossbar on the correct angle the puck would deflect upward and stick in the ceiling insulation. True story."

That was back in the mid-1980s. For two seasons, Campbell's hockey journey took him back to where it all began for him—his hometown of New Waterford, on Cape Breton Island. At the tail end of the 1970s, fresh off leading New Waterford to a Nova Scotia provincial Midget championship, Bruce was in his first year of Junior, lighting it up for the New Waterford Junior A Jets. "My girlfriend today was a big fan back in the day. She still says, 'Oh my God, that was a thing to do back in the seventies, to go watch Brucey play hockey,'" says Campbell.

These days, "Brucey" is just Bruce, and he still lives in New Waterford, where he grew up in a family of twelve. Like a lot of towns in industrial Cape Breton, New Waterford, a twenty-five-minute drive north of Sydney, is a lot smaller than it used to be. The population used to be ten thousand-plus; these days it's a little under seven thousand. The coal mines have been closed for years and things aren't so shiny and new anymore. In March 2022, the headline in the local newspaper, the *Cape Breton Post*, cut right to the chase: "New Waterford and District Community Centre Needs Support, Major Upgrades to Stay Open."

Back in 1978, "the New Waterford Rink" was only a few years old and Campbell was the hockey superstar in the bustling little town. "We were filling the rinks with Junior hockey at that time. I used to joke that the safest place to be at a Junior game was on the ice. Our fans played rough," says Bruce. "The coal miners? They'd be saying, 'New Waterford's going to beat the Bay [Glace Bay] tonight!' Then the plant people from Sydney would say, or sometimes shout, 'Sydney's going to win!' The rivalries were huge back then and it showed in the attendance because the rinks were always full."

On the ice it was town against town. The mines in New Waterford were pumping out coal. The mines would also pump out the paycheques, which was all good for Campbell and the Junior A Jets: "Payday was Thursday in the coal mines and our home games were on Thursday nights. You could imagine the emotion in the stands. You'd look in the bleachers after a whistle and there'd be a donnybrook taking place."

In between the fighting miners, the kids of New Waterford

would also jam into the rink. Huddled under the clouds of cigarette smoke, it was a chance for the town's youngest hockey connoisseurs to see the real-life game up close. There was a kid from just outside of town who started to hear about this Brucey fellow, and he decided to see for himself. "My older brother would talk about Bruce all the time," says Patrick Lewis, now in his fifties. "We lived on the outskirts of New Waterford in a community called River Ryan. My father and uncle ran a service station, and you'd hear the older guys coming in to hang out and they'd be talking about Bruce."

They'd talk about Bruce all the time because he scored all the time: 88 goals in 30 games for the Jets in the 1978–79 season. No one had ever scored more in the Eastern Junior A Hockey League. Bruce's 147 points were a league record. Patrick tells me over the phone, "Everybody would say, 'Yeah, he's gonna make it to the NHL.' It was expected. He was a step above the other guys on the ice."

The following season, Bruce left his hometown for the first time and took his hockey talents to PEI for another season of record-setting results: 77 goals and 130 points in 40 games for the North River North Stars. The previous season, when he played in New Waterford, Bruce was runner-up for Canadian Junior A Player of the Year; in 1980, he won it. (One of the other three finalists for the award in 1980 was Brent Sutter—yes, that Brent Sutter, who played more than 1,000 games in the NHL and won two Stanley Cups with the New York Islanders.) The award was handed out as part of the festivities during that year's Centennial Cup tournament. His team didn't make it to the tournament, but Bruce did, traveling to North York, Ontario, just north of Toronto, as a guest to accept the award. He then sat back and watched Brent Sutter and the Red Deer Rustlers win the 1980 Canadian championship.

During that tournament, pro hockey finally tapped the kid from Cape Breton Island—that was not necessarily a good thing. "I think the biggest mistake I made in my hockey career was when I was there at the nationals," says Bruce. "A representative from the Winnipeg Jets came to me and said, 'Congratulations on winning the award. Would you like to come to Jets training camp?' And here I am from New Waterford, not even playing in this tournament, and somebody's invited me to an NHL camp! What do you think I did?"

The kid from Cape Breton could not believe his ears. Pro hockey was right in front of him! "I said, 'Sure. I'd love to go to camp.' So, he [the Jets rep] pulls out an ATO [Amateur Tryout Agreement]. I'm sitting there with him, and I sign it."

Campbell did not have an agent. Little did he know that when he signed the ATO he lost a ton of options. It's likely that many other NHL teams would have had him on their radar for the 1980 NHL Draft, but now he was ineligible because he had already signed the ATO with Winnipeg. Brent Sutter was drafted seventeenth overall in that very draft, which makes you wonder what might have been. "When I spoke to people after that they all said, 'No, you didn't sign, you didn't sign! You could've gone into the draft. You could've held out. You could've had an agent. You could've said, *I'm the Canadian Junior Player of the Year. I'm not going to camp unless I have a contract.*' All those things. When I look back, that was a major mistake I made," Bruce reminisces. "What I should've said was, 'I'll go home for the summer, talk to some hockey people from the local area, and get some guidance.' But there were no agents back there at the time. So, you take a kid from New Waterford and say to him, 'Would you like to come to the NHL camp?' Well, I almost jumped out of my seat!"

Bruce spent his summer back home in Cape Breton before he made his way to Winnipeg Jets camp. Not surprisingly, since he was still only nineteen, he didn't make the team out of camp. The Jets' general manager, the legendary John Ferguson Sr.—a five-time Stanley Cup champion with the Montreal Canadiens and the assistant coach for Team Canada 1972—had a plan for the young Cape Bretoner.

"John said to me, 'The strength of your game is scoring and offence, but you need some seasoning on the defensive side. We'd like to send you to Bowling Green University,'" Bruce recalls. Bowling Green was one of top-ranked schools in American college hockey. One of their top scorers was future NHLer George McPhee. Brian MacLellan, another forward on the team, went on to play 606 NHL regular season games.

Bruce had no interest in hitting the books. He was about to make what he calls another mistake: "Of course, here I am, nineteen years old, and my goal is not to go to university. I want to play hockey. Pro hockey. Again, you look back, that could've been a major mistake, too. Now I know Bowling Green is a renowned university, but then I did not, which is too bad. They ended up winning the nationals maybe one or two years after the Jets wanted to send me there. So, I kind of refused." He pauses for a moment. "Actually, I said no altogether. The Jets said, 'If you're not going to go to Bowling Green then we're going to release you.' I ended up coming home."

Campbell went back to New Waterford, where just a couple of seasons earlier he was the star for the Junior A Jets. The Winnipeg Jets didn't work out and he didn't want to play college hockey, so what was next? He had no intention of sitting at home. Fortunately, that's when one of the toughest men to ever suit up in the NHL made a house call to New Waterford.

Forbes Kennedy looks tough, and he is. His name even sounds tough. The back of his 1957–58 rookie card lists him at 5'8" and 168 pounds. It also says he was born in Dorchester, New Brunswick. That makes sense. Dorchester is a prison town, and Forbes, or Forbie as he is better known, took no prisoners on the ice. In an era when Maritimers were often passed over, Forbie somehow made it all the way to the NHL and stuck around long enough to rack up a very tidy 888 career penalty minutes in 603 NHL regular season games.

But Forbie Kennedy is perhaps best known for the final game of his career. On April 2, 1969, he single-handedly brought the Boston Garden to the brink of a near riot. Forbie, who was innocently hanging out in front of the Boston net, took a slash from Boston goalie Gerry Cheevers. Forbie went wild—he wanted a piece of the Bruins goalie, and he got it, slugging the tender down to the ice. From there it was a full-on brawl, gloves and fists everywhere. Linesman George Ashley, trying to play the peacemaker, attempted to calm Forbie down. Forbie punched Ashley to the ice, too, then tangled with Cheevers for round two. Bruins player John "Pie" McKenzie and backup goalie Eddie Johnston grabbed at Forbie, and a fan reached over the glass and punched Forbie on the top of his head. Forbie somehow got free to go one-on-one with McKenzie. In the end, Forbie ended the game with 38 penalty minutes, a single-game record at the time, a four-game suspension, and a $1,000 fine for punching Ashley. As Forbie told CBC's *Hockey Day in Canada* in 2012, with a twinkle in his eye, "She was a tough night."

A little over a decade later, Forbie was in the Campbell house in New Waterford, looking to take Bruce with him to—of all places—Newfoundland. Forbie, who had coached against Bruce the previous season in PEI, was the new head coach of the Corner Brook Royals of the Newfoundland Senior Hockey League. "Forbes came to the house and stayed overnight with my parents and us. He convinced me to go to Corner Brook," says Bruce.

Newfoundland is a long way from the NHL. Bruce didn't know a thing about the Newfoundland League, but he would soon learn that it paid well, had a lot of offence, and especially loved tough hockey. The league was shot through with under-the-radar players and former pros, and in particular, a certain type of former pro: the tough guy.

Bruce, as per his custom, did his thing on the ice and was named league MVP. But when it comes time to tell tales about the Newfoundland League—and Bruce has lots of them—it's not the goals and assists, but the legendary toughies on the ice on the Rock. "When people ask me about the Newfoundland Senior League it seems like the first thing that comes out of my mouth is the magnitude of the physical play," he says. "Stan Hennigar, Jeff Leverman, Kevin Morrison, Serge and Mario Roberge—it seems like I'm always telling stories about those guys. It's never about me scoring a goal in overtime or this guy getting a hat trick or that guy scoring fifty goals."

One thing that Bruce immediately noticed upon his arrival in Newfoundland: the crowds never arrived late. In town after town, from Corner Brook to Gander to Smith Falls to Stephenville, and all stops in between, the warm-up was one of the main events of the evening. "I'd say to myself, why are these rinks sold out for the warm-up? I found out soon. There were no referees on the ice for warm-up. No video cameras. There were all kinds of . . . she-nanigans," Bruce explains.

"Let me give an example. Jeff Leverman would be skating around the ice—you must have heard of Jeff Leverman? He'd be all Vaseline'd up. His knuckles would be taped up, which you were allowed to do back then—you could tape your wrists and your hands right up to the knuckles. And Jeff would be skating around just like you'd see in *Slap Shot*. He'd be pointing his stick down at the other team. And if you crossed the red line there would be a donnybrook, and I was like . . . oh my God. You had to button your helmet up in the warm-up. Now you don't wear helmets. We had to button ours up."

In the deep mines of hockey history, there are some notorious names: Goldie Goldthorpe, Steve Durbano, "Battleship" Bob Kelly, and one Gordie "Machine Gun" Gallant. Listed at 5'11" and 165 pounds, Gallant ranks sixth in the WHA for penalty minutes. The Minnesota Fighting Saints once kicked him off the team for punching head coach Harry Neale—Gordie was forty-five minutes late for curfew and didn't like that Harry had called to check on him. A few years after that dustup, Gordie was doing his thing in Newfoundland. Bruce remembers one particular night: "Gordie came out with boxing gloves on in the warm-up. He was with Grand Falls. True story. He was skating around the warm-up with all his equipment on and he had boxing gloves on with his hockey stick. Now if that wouldn't wanna make someone quit hockey, just what the fuck am I into here?

"I was fortunate to play with Gordie for a season and I played against him for a season," Bruce continues. "You know a guy is tough when he is your teammate and you're still afraid of him.

Think about that for a second. Now imagine being on the *other* team."

The kid from New Waterford more than survived that first year on the Rock. He led the Royals with 42 goals and 79 points in only 32 regular season games. Those numbers caught the attention of the Quebec Nordiques. Some might consider it a strange route to the pros, Newfoundland to the NHL, but Bruce was once again on the edge of making it in the pro game. He hung out with the Nordiques and their American Hockey League farm club, the Fredericton Express, for six weeks: "I was playing on a regular basis but there was no contract for me. Jacques Demers was the coach [in Fredericton]. He didn't know what to do with me." The Nordiques had twenty-five contracts signed with the big club and another twenty-five signed with the AHL club, so the organization was not in a position to give out more. Campbell created a problem for the Nordiques and their top farm club by doing what he always did: scoring goals. As Demers told Fredericton newspaper the *Daily Gleaner* after an Express exhibition game: "The net is like an ocean to him. Give him an inch and it's in the net."

Bruce's scoring didn't make a difference. He'd always put up the numbers and was now caught in another numbers game. "I had scored a hat trick in an exhibition game against Sherbrooke, I believe," he says. "My teammates were saying to me, 'Did you sign a contract?' I said no. They said, 'You got to get your ass out of here! What's gonna happen is you're going to get injured or something and they're just going to put you on the bus and send you home.' I was getting pissed. I told Jacques I needed a decision."

Bruce was living on thirty-seven dollars a day in meal money from the Nordiques and the Express. He wanted a deal, so

Demers offered Bruce a twenty-five-game tryout contract with the Express. Bruce refused the offer and instead went back to Newfoundland, where he knew he could earn more money. The Newfoundland League paid well, but it was still a hockey wilderness compared to Fredericton: "That was another mistake I made. I should've taken the twenty-five games and see what came out of it." That was Bruce's last shot at the NHL.

Bruce, playing for Grand Falls, won the Newfoundland scoring title that season, and again the following season playing for the Stephenville Jets. He set a provincial record with 40 goals and won the league scoring title with 72 points.

But then it was time to come home. Bruce played both the 1983–84 and 1985–86 seasons for the New Waterford Cavaliers of the Nova Scotia Senior Hockey League. He sandwiched another season in Newfoundland in between. Just like his time with the Junior Jets, he was a scoring star with the Senior Cavaliers. At one point in his first season back home, he racked up 56 points in a ten-game stretch. And, of course, he won the scoring title. The kids who first watched him with the Jets were now teenagers; there was a whole new crop of young hockey fans to impress. "Bruce being Bruce, he was just at another level compared to everybody else. He just controlled the play. Wayne Gretzky is Wayne Gretzky, sure, but Bruce Campbell was my Wayne Gretzky—everybody's Gretzky—in New Waterford," says Steve MacKenzie, who watched Bruce play for the Cavs through his nine-year-old eyes.

By the end of the 1986 season, Bruce was firmly entrenched as a local legend. He took his show on the road for two more seasons, playing in Dartmouth and in Pictou County, Nova Scotia. It was Senior hockey or bust for the near thirty-year-old. Or was it?

KEN REID'S HOMETOWN HOCKEY HEROES

After a season of Senior hockey in Pictou County, where he played for the legendary Hugh Sim (and played mini sticks with Hughie's kids; one of them, Jon, went on to play 469 NHL games and win a Stanley Cup with the Dallas Stars), Campbell finally decided to hit the books. Years after turning down the chance to go to Bowling Green, Bruce got another chance to play university hockey. The University College of Cape Breton, locally known as UCCB (and known today as Cape Breton University), was about to launch its first season in the Atlantic University League. The coach was Bucky Buchanan. Looking around the Island, he saw the perfect captain for his team.

There was just one problem: Bruce Campbell was twenty-eight years old. He wasn't exactly Rodney Dangerfield *Back to School* old, but he wasn't a kid, either. Buchanan had to fight to get permission for Bruce to suit up for the Capers. "The league made a stink because they were saying there's no way that a twenty-eight-year-old guy who's played pro hockey should be allowed to come back [to play university hockey]. It didn't look like I was going to be allowed to play after committing to go so then it became a discriminatory thing," says Bruce. "They [the team] said, 'The guy is going to university and he's like anybody else. Why would he not be allowed to play, no matter if he's fifty years old? Bucky had to fight that. Apparently, a rule was passed that I was allowed to play. Bucky, when he talks to me these days, says, 'I'll always remember the Bruce Campbell rule.'"

The "Bruce Campbell rule" is not unheard-of today. According to current Acadia University hockey coach Darren Burns, who suited up for Acadia in the AUAA in the mid-1990s, the rule supposedly stated a player had to start playing in the AUAA before the age of twenty-five. No matter, Bruce captained the

Capers for four seasons starting in fall 1987. He ended up graduating with a bachelor of arts in community studies.

After that, Bruce played what he calls "scrub hockey"—rec league with his buddies. And that's where our story ends, right? How about another twist. In 1987, Sydney, Nova Scotia, hosted the Canada Games. One of the city's key bonuses for hosting Canada's best young athletes was the building of Centre 200, a new sports and entertainment facility in the heart of the city. It was a beautiful building, seating just over four thousand; the perfect kind of building for any good team, say, for example, an American Hockey League team.

And voila! The Cape Breton Oilers arrived on the scene for fall 1988. Until the St. John's Maple Leafs joined the league in 1991, Sydney was the most remote post in the AHL, and because of this it became a problem for the Oilers to get players to Sydney at a moment's notice. Dave Andrews, a local boy who went on to become the commissioner of the AHL, was the Cape Breton Oilers' general manager in the early 1990s. During the 1991 season, when the Oilers were in need of a player, Andrews placed a call to the area's most famous recent university-hockey-playing graduate. "They used to say I played scrub hockey on Tuesday nights and then I played with the Cape Breton Oilers on Wednesday nights," Bruce chuckles.

All these years later, now in this thirties, Bruce Campbell was a step below the NHL. Sure, he was just filling a spot on the roster, but he was sharing a dressing room with players like Shaun Van Allen and Steven Rice, who themselves would go on to long NHL careers. He's casual about it. He even dropped back to play on the blue line in the AHL, after all those years of being a top scoring forward. Bruce says, "I kept myself in good shape and

I was always on the ice. So instead of calling down to the East Coast League or calling around the country to get utility players, they'd call me. I was living in the area. They'd say, 'We have a three-week injury—this guy hurt his shoulder—can you play for three weeks?' I went from elite scoring forward to a defenceman, which is not easy to do at the AHL level."

Over two seasons Bruce ended up suiting up for thirteen AHL games. He never did score a goal, but he did get two assists. The Oilers paid him three hundred dollars a game, which was pretty good coin back in those days, and, as a plus, he'd join them for road trips. Every once in a while, the old fella in the dressing room would find himself under the spotlight again, like one night when the Oilers made the trip east to the Rock to face off against the St. John's Maple Leafs: "I had played there in the Senior leagues and the guys on the Cape Breton Oilers weren't really aware of the magnitude of the Newfoundland League or the success I had with them. Funny story—after a game, all the reporters wanted to talk to me. The other players [with the Oilers], who called me 'Soupy,' were saying, 'Why are all the reporters looking for Soupy? He only played twelve minutes tonight.'"

That question was answered for the team the next day when they saw Soupy on the front page of the sports section. "The boys were like, 'Oh fuck, Soupy. We didn't realize!' And I said, 'Yeah, I played a little bit.' I wasn't gonna start bragging to them that I did this, I did that," says Bruce. "I just kind of let the story go. They picked up the paper the next day and they said, 'Okay, we get it.'"

When Campbell played a home game for the Oilers, it was the place to be for anyone who grew up in New Waterford. Steve MacKenzie, whose aunt had married Bruce's father, would get the inside scoop on when the local hero was going to suit up:

"My aunt would call and tell us Bruce is playing tonight for Cape Breton. I'd say, 'Dad, we got to go.' I was sixteen or seventeen, a huge Edmonton Oilers fan, and we go just to watch Bruce play—it was awesome. When Bruce would get called up, you'd think, oh my God, Bruce is playing one step away from the NHL. It was a huge deal."

Those thirteen games with the Cape Breton Oilers would be the last time fans would see Bruce on the ice as a player at Centre 200. Bruce went on to coach Junior B in the area. Major Junior hockey came to Sydney in 1997 and Bruce signed on as an assistant coach with the Cape Breton Screaming Eagles; he'd jump into the play from time to time when the team scrimmaged. The "old guy," almost forty, would skate with the kids, and in typical Bruce Campbell fashion, he would turn heads. Bruce's brother Glen, the youngest of the twelve siblings, who to this day is known in New Waterford as being Bruce's little brother, or Mike's son (their father also was a great hockey player), was not surprised when Danny Dube, head coach of the Screaming Eagles, filled him in on what went down at practice one day: "Dube told me a scout was at the rink watching a scrimmage and asked Danny, 'Holy cow, who is that?' And Dube says, 'That's the assistant coach, man. He's thirty-something years old. You can't draft him.'"

Bruce Campbell still had it. He could still skate and more than hold his own with a Major Junior team. And the story of Bruce Campbell still had one more act. In 1998, the town of Truro, Nova Scotia, hosted the Allan Cup—the Canadian Senior hockey championship. Truro reached out to the now forty-something Campbell, who was still an assistant coach with the Screaming Eagles. They wanted to know, if the Eagles went out early in the spring, could Bruce make it to Truro to play in the Allan Cup?

"Danny Dube told me, 'You need your head examined. You just coached and traveled all over the country for eight months,'" says Bruce. "I skated with our team a lot. I put my equipment on when I could, and I always played scrub hockey in the evenings. In my head I knew I could play in the Allan Cup because I could still skate and my body weight was good. But Danny reminded me it's going to be body contact and I hadn't played body contact for the last number of years."

Danny made a valid point: a forty-year-old who hadn't played competitive hockey in years shouldn't just step on the ice for the Allan Cup. But Bruce played and he did just fine: "I contributed, but I wasn't the guy who made the difference." When it ended, he and the Truro Bearcats were Allan Cup champions. The team was inducted into the Nova Scotia Sport Hall of Fame. "I will say, once it was over, I was relieved because it was pretty intense," Bruce laughs.

Bruce was inducted into the New Waterford & District Sports Heritage Hall of Fame in August 2015. He is also a member of the Cape Breton Sport Hall of Fame. He was the head coach of the Screaming Eagles for a season and a half after he won the Allan Cup, and he still plays. "Bruce became pretty difficult to play against in his older age, I guess," says Steve MacKenzie, who still sees Bruce when he makes his way home to New Waterford from his current home in Dartmouth, Nova Scotia. "Nobody wanted to play with Bruce anymore because he took it too seriously. He is still very competitive and still quite good. Beer league guys just go out and want to skate around and go drink beer for a couple hours."

Hey, when you still got it, you still got it. Bruce still lives in New Waterford. And there's a new generation of Campbells running around the ice. Glen's son, Andrew, is now a high-level player, a given with Bruce coaching him on the outdoor rink. "My son is only sixteen—sometimes I feel for him," begins Glen, "because the Campbell name is sort of known around here for hockey. My son will introduce himself, 'I'm Andrew Campbell, from New Waterford.' People will say, 'Are you any relation to Bruce Campbell?' He proudly says yes—he loves it. But sometimes I feel that they're expecting huge things from him."

Andrew is known as Bruce's nephew and at one time Bruce was known as Mike's son. That's just how it goes. But Bruce made his own name in hockey, and maybe Andrew will, too. It doesn't seem to matter to the Campbell family. "It was really cool to be Bruce's little brother," says Glen. "It still is. We're recognized because we have such a big family, and because of my dad. I'm always Bruce Campbell's brother or Mike Campbell's son, but I've never minded it one bit because I'm proud to be associated with my brother."

In a small town, it's also good for business. Glen says, "I'm a lawyer. All joking aside, it actually helps in my business. People will call and say, 'Oh, I know Bruce. I used to play hockey with him.' I suspect it's part of the reason they're calling me."

Bruce and Glen's father, Mike Campbell, played hockey until he was ninety-three years old. You can see where Bruce gets it from. "It means everything. It still seems to be what I'm remembered for today. I did play lots of hockey after playing here in New Waterford, but it seems like, oh my God, you know, back in the day it was the thing to do," says Bruce.

Maybe Bruce didn't know it then, but he was a big deal in town. He tells me that perhaps he took that time for granted, all those times he was thrilling New Waterford. He's a humble guy, which happens when you are one of twelve kids. He's not one to sit around and brag, going into detail only when the occasional reporter calls. Now he can sit back and enjoy his spot as New Waterford's hockey legend. "One thing about a small town, you never really thought you were anything," he says. "But when you get older, it's nice to sit back and reflect and say, 'You know, I guess I was pretty good at it.'"

Bruce during his days with the New Waterford Jets.

CHAPTER 3

Mike "Pinky" Gallant

Summerside, Prince Edward Island

"Just rights, rights, rights, rights, rights, rights from Pinky. Just one right after another, after another, after another. Now he's taking rights, too. I might've seen Pinky's knee buckle once or twice. It would be his right knee that I would see buckle. But he never went down." That is how George Matthews described the legendary Prince Edward Island Junior Hockey League fights between Summerside's Mike "Pinky" Gallant and Sherwood-Parkdale's Steve Gallant (yes, the same Steve Gallant in chapter 1 who went on to play in Newfoundland). The Gallants weren't related, and that's a good thing, because two relatives should never do what they used to do to each other on the ice in the late 1970s.

"There would be an event every game," Matthews continues. "They would match up and it was showtime. They didn't necessarily wait and hit one another in the corner. No, it was a preplanned event that was going to happen at some point in the game. There wasn't a cluster of players to pull sweaters apart. These two guys were going to go at it."

George Matthews knows a thing or two about hockey. He has

called play-by-play for close to 3,000 games. His career started in PEI and took him all the way to the NHL. He was the first radio voice of the Columbus Blue Jackets; he spent thirteen seasons in their broadcast booth. He did the play-by-play for over 1,000 NHL games. From his perch high above the ice, he has witnessed some legendary NHL gladiators do battle: Bob Probert, Tie Domi, Chris Simon, Donald Brashear, and on and on. Matthews was on the mic when Jody Shelley began his rise to Columbus folk hero. On January 10, 2002, Shelley, who was just a rookie, fought the veteran Probert three times in one game. It cemented Shelley in Blue Jackets history, but it was nothing Matthews hadn't seen before.

"I used to see Jody Shelley all the time in the Blue Jackets dressing room. I'd say, 'Jody, you think you're tough? I got a guy back on the East Coast. I've never seen him lose a fight in Junior or Senior hockey.' Jody and I would laugh and joke, but Pinky was scared of nobody and would challenge a player when the situation warranted it. Pinky wasn't necessarily a goon. He considered himself a hockey player. But I never saw him lose a fight. He fought all the tough guys. He might take fifty rights in a fight but he's going to get the fifty-first."

In his Junior days, Pinky made an impression on the team's stick boy. Like a lot of kids in Summerside, Gerard Gallant (no relation to Pinky) didn't necessarily dream of playing in the NHL; he just wanted to play for the Junior A Summerside Crystals. In the late seventies, the town was about thirteen thousand people and, along with many of the kids, Gerard spent his time at the Boys and Girls Club, the ball fields, and Cahill Stadium.

Cahill Stadium was the epicenter of the town, a classic old barn that even had a bowling alley attached to it. When the hockey season rolled around, it was the place to be and in the days of the Summerside Junior A Crystals, Mike "Pinky" Gallant often took centre stage. "The fights were incredible. We all knew Pinky and Stevie were going to fight. Everybody knew. Both guys were willing to do it and happy to do it and they enjoyed doing what they were doing. Everybody knew on Saturday night that come game time Sunday, whether the game was in Charlottetown or in Summerside, that there were going to be two or three fights with Pinky and Stevie. They pretty much fought themselves most of the time," says Gerard, who grew up just a couple of blocks away from Pinky's house in Summerside (the origin of the nickname: Pinky lived in a pink house).

During our call, Gerard tells me: "The biggest thing I remember is I wanted to play on that team. He fought three times every Sunday afternoon. He was the toughest guy in the league."

Gerard never did get to play for the Crystals. He skipped that level. Also known as "Turk" around the Island and in the hockey world, Gerard was most recently the head coach of the New York Rangers. He played 615 regular season games in the NHL and another 58 in the playoffs. He could score and he was tough—Gallant had 480 points in his regular season career to go along with 1,674 penalty minutes. He spent the first nine seasons of his NHL career with the Detroit Red Wings, playing often on a line with future Hall of Famer Steve Yzerman. Gallant was also a fair player, just like Pinky, but with more skill that brought him all the way to the NHL.

"One hundred percent," says Matthews. "Now, Gerard had greater finish to his game, and that's why he made it to the NHL, but all the other stuff, the toughness, the drive, the other variables that people love about a hockey player, Mike 'Pinky' Gallant and Gerard Gallant would be similar."

Pinky wasn't just a tough guy. He could score goals and set them up as well. But his toughness gave him a lot of room on the ice. Once his Junior career wrapped up, he went on to play Senior hockey on the Island. The key word here is *Island*. This was back in the late 1970s and through the 1980s, before the Confederation Bridge connected PEI to the mainland. During the long PEI winters, there were times when, hard as you might try, you could not get out of the province, and it made for a unique lifestyle and a unique hockey experience in the Junior or Senior ranks.

"On PEI there were some terrific rivalries back then," says Matthews. "Summerside and Charlottetown, when they were closer in terms of population size, would be like Montreal against Toronto. Tignish and O'Leary would be like the Yankees and the Red Sox. What perhaps took them up another notch is that when you live on an island, the island is, to the people who live on it, the world. In those days there was just a boat to get across. You took great pride in representing your community."

That is the essence of the great rivalries in the good old days of Senior hockey on PEI. In the 1980s a lot of young men didn't leave their hometowns. Unlike today, a lot of young people didn't leave the province—they stuck around, and both made their living and competed on the Island. During the cold winter months, young men would drive from town to town to play Senior hockey. Bill MacKendrick is one of the biggest hockey fans you can find on PEI or just about anywhere else. He helped his hometown of O'Leary win the 2017 Kraft Hockeyville title as the most passionate hockey town in Canada. Bill can still list off the teams from the golden era of Senior hockey on his Island: "The Tignish Aces, they always had a strong team in that league. O'Leary's population is 860 and they had a team. Alberton had teams periodically.

Tyne Valley only had a population of 400 but they had teams in the Senior leagues."

Bill saw a lot of Senior games in his day and got to see Pinky do his thing. "I had a neighbour who was hit by Pinky very hard, and he had a back injury, but I wasn't at that game, unfortunately. Pinky was one of the greatest players I've seen play. He was tough. He was a great goal scorer, but he could play the game the way it was meant to be played—tough."

Mike McIver was a tough player coming out of the Junior ranks when he took his skills to the PEI Senior circuit in the early 1980s, joining the Borden Ramparts. Borden was the "ferry town" on the western end of the Island; from there, you could hop on the boat and head to the mainland. Pinky was already a member of the team when the younger McIver joined the squad. Mike knew he was going to meet one of the toughest players on the Island, but he also knew he was going to meet one of the nicest guys off the ice. One thing you keep hearing about Pinky Gallant: as tough as he was on the ice, he was just as kind off it. "I had a real good friend of mine who played Senior with him before I did," says Mike. "My friend never knew Pinky either and he was going to play with the Borden Ramparts. Pinky was on the team. My friend was half-intimidated going into the dressing room. I remember my friend telling me, and I will remember it as long as I live, 'I couldn't believe how polite and mild-mannered Pinky was. Everything was please and thank you.' You wouldn't know Pinky was the same person when he stepped on the ice."

When Mike started playing with Pinky, he got to see his kindness and toughness up close. One night in O'Leary things got a little out of hand. The O'Leary barn can be intimidating. All the stands are on one side of the ice, unlike most small rinks, where fans of one team would be opposite the fans of the other. With everyone mixed in the stands, things could get a little rowdy. If things started heating up on the ice, they could spill over into the stands, with both the fans and sometimes the players involved. So, one night in O'Leary, the fans, including one very unlucky one, became part of the storyline.

"The fans are leaning right over the boards," says Mike, "and somebody took a punch at Pinky. I just happened to be right there, and I grabbed the fan by the pants. I was holding him until Pinky could get over the boards, but I let the fan go and he ran right into the old wall and pillar that held the rink up. And then Pinky, he got ahold of him, and beat the shit out of him."

The lesson here is do not mess with Pinky Gallant. But the toughness was confined to the rink, even if a fan wanted a piece of the players off the ice, say in the parking lot. "Especially up in Tignish," says Mike. "But Pinky wasn't involved. A bunch of kids were outside waiting for the players, but [instead] the Tignish goalie came out and put the run to them and nothing really happened. But I remember getting chased off the ice up in Tignish by the fans and the referees. It was just crazy sometimes."

It's a good thing Pinky and Mike hit it off so well. While they were teammates, Pinky started dating Mike's sister Patricia. That was not a problem at all. The two became best friends and eventually brothers-in-law. At times, they would even play Senior hockey against each other. Pinky went on to play Senior in Summerside for a time, which meant that the two pals, both tough as nails, would have to face off against each other. But they never dropped the gloves, even though one die-hard fan wanted to see them go. "Pinky's dad always, always wanted us to fight, just to see who would win," Mike laughs. "It would never have happened. He was tough. We had a lot of laughs over it."

About twenty-five years after Pinky Gallant's Senior hockey days wrapped up, his son Brett Gallant sat alone in the penalty box at Nassau Veterans Memorial Coliseum in Uniondale, New York. He had fought his way to get there (literally). Brett Gallant was maybe a little bigger than his father at six feet and 190 pounds, but by hockey tough-guy standards he was no giant. Nor was he a blue-chip prospect. But there he was, alone in the penalty box, seconds after his first NHL fight in his first NHL game, with the New York Islanders.

Brett Gallant had just dropped the gloves with Ottawa Senators tough guy Matt Kassian, nine minutes and fifty-nine seconds into his NHL debut. The fight did not last long. Gallant's first punch connected with Kassian's chin and sent the six-foot-four, 234-pounder to the ice. "Gallant finishes about as quickly as Muhammad Ali finished Sonny Liston in their second fight," the play-by-play announcer screamed. A few seconds later, Gallant sat stoically in the penalty box. Up in the stands his parents, Pinky and Patricia, were looking on. Brett had made it all the way to the best league in the world. He played it cool when he was interviewed after the first period. The interviewer started things off by calling him Brent. This did not faze Gallant at all. He was locked into hockey interview mode.

"Brent, listen, you're the envy of every young guy who's dreaming about playing in the National Hockey League. How's it been after twenty minutes of play?"

This rookie made a veteran move. He stuck to the clichés: "You know, we're having a good game. We're getting in on the forecheck. We're getting shots on net. That's what a bigger part of our game tonight was. For me I got a hit on my first shift, and I feel pretty good."

Then the clichés disappear. When "Brent" is asked about who's responsible for him being in the NHL, he gives the answer every young player dreams of giving. "I could sit here and thank a lot of people, and I know most kids would say this, but it is definitely my parents. My mother and my father carting me everywhere. Me and my brothers. They're definitely my biggest influences." Pinky's kid was an NHLer.

Brett was one of the three Gallant boys: the middle, between older brother Brad and younger brother Alex. They have a half sister, Jennifer, as well. As for Brad, Brett, and Alex, "To this day we're all kind of considered Pinky's boys," says Alex.

All three played pro hockey. Brad had a brief pro career after playing university hockey at St. Thomas in Fredericton, New Brunswick. Brett made it all the way to the NHL for four games, and Alex has carved out a long pro career as one of the toughest players in the AHL. All three grew up playing on some of the same rinks their father once played in during his glory days: "Every time we'd be going up to western PEI, someone would always say, 'You're Pinky's son! He had a lot of wars in this building.'"

"Senior hockey was huge back then; I definitely heard lots of stories around the rink as a kid," says Alex.

He'd also keep hearing about the legendary scraps of Gallant versus Gallant. Stevie versus Pinky. The tilts George Matthews and Gerard Gallant still talk about. Anyone—and I mean anyone—who was in Junior or Senior hockey in PEI in the late 1970s or '80s tells these stories. "I don't know how many goals they had, but when people talk about Dad, they bring up Stevie Gallant all the time, the total battles Dad and Stevie had. They'd say Stevie might win one night, Pinky might win the next night, but every time was an all-out brawl," says Alex.

One of the great things about PEI is its sense of community. Everyone knows everyone else, or at least is not too far removed from someone across town or even across PEI. "Stevie's a great man," says Alex. "I ran into him this summer. He's a retired cop. Stevie had a lot of good stuff to say about the wars he and my dad used to have."

When he was raising his boys, Pinky and his wife, Patricia, were like most other parents, doing anything they could to give their kids every opportunity they needed, on and off the ice. Pinky hung up the skates and helped raise the kids. Between working, reffing, and being a dad, Pinky was also coaching the boys: "We'd be in four or five hockey camps in the summer. We lived in the rinks. That's what we loved. That was their passion, but Mom and Dad weren't crazy hockey parents. Obviously, none of us were studs growing up or anything. We just kind of worked hard. But they weren't the kind of parents who said, 'Hey, my kids are going to the NHL.' They didn't think that way at all. They just said if it happens, it happens."

It happened for Brett. It could still happen for Alex. All three Gallant boys did end up following in their father's footsteps and playing Junior A hockey in Summerside. And they played much like their father did. In a combined 188 games the boys played for the Western Capitals, they put up 902 penalty minutes: an average of almost five minutes in penalties per game. The boys played the same way when they suited up in the Quebec Major Junior Hockey League and into pro: "You know, both of those boys [Alex and Brett], they're not big kids. They might be 190 pounds at the most," says Gerard Gallant. "They're five eleven, maybe six feet.

They do it the hard way and they don't mind doing it. They love what they're doing, and I think they got that from their father. No nonsense. Ever."

The Gallant boys could go, the Gallant boys could throw. It was rock-'em sock-'em, Gallant-style, on PEI all over again. "Dad told me this so many times and I still to this day make sure I do this—if you beat me once I'm coming right back. That's one thing everyone knew about Dad. They almost didn't want to beat him because they knew that if they beat Dad, he's coming out of the box and he's coming after you. I've been beat a few times for sure. I'll never forget Dad saying, 'If you beat me, it's a bad thing because you know I'm coming back until I beat you. I'm going to keep fighting.' That's something that he instilled in me. Big-time. And that's something I always kind of take pride in. It's the way I think, too," says Alex.

Alex Gallant's Junior days came to an end after Summerside's 2012–13 season. He needed shoulder surgery before figuring out his next move. Turning pro? As Alex told me on our call, agents weren't knocking down his door. So Pinky Gallant became a hockey agent. He was going to get his kid into the pros, somehow and somewhere.

"Dad was talking to a few East Coast teams and a few CHL [Canadian Hockey League] teams at the time and with the Southern Professional Hockey League. I came off shoulder surgery, so I didn't start that season until November. Coming off surgery, a lot of teams were scared off by the insurance. This meant I had trouble finding a college job. I couldn't find a job anywhere. Dad hit the phones, and he got me a three-game tryout in Columbus, Georgia."

The SPHL was a long way from the NHL, a long way from home, and the pay wasn't exactly going to put Alex over the top.

"I'm thinking, 'I'm playing pro hockey! This is awesome. I'm going to finally start to make some money.' I made seventy-five bucks per game."

That's a combined $225, minus taxes, to head south and (more than likely) take a few punches, but hey, it was a shot. "Dad said, 'Alex, it's just a stepping-stone. You won't be there long if you just bury your head and put the work in.' And he was right."

Alex Gallant went to work. His SPHL team was not affiliated with any East Coast Hockey League teams, so he was not going to get a call-up that season. He didn't find that out until the end of the year. Turns out if he was going to cut it in pro hockey, he'd be spending his first season in Columbus. That was just fine. "To be honest, it was one of my favourite years of hockey," Alex says. "We had an amazing group. We lost in the finals. I got to play lots down there, so it helped me grow as a player, but it also helped me become a lot better fighter, too. I think I got twenty-eight fights that year. It was mayhem."

The fans in Georgia liked the scraps, just like the fans in PEI thirty-five years before. "It was crazy, absolutely crazy. Mom and Dad came down a couple of times. I remember Dad always would say after the games that he loved it. The fans were there for the fights. They'd be on their feet yelling and screaming. You had big army nights down there. The military guys would be going crazy. I'm glad Dad got to experience that, and my mom got to experience that. Years later, Dad kept saying how that was the coolest atmosphere he had seen. It was pretty special. There were some wild barns down there."

Alex Gallant put in the time and elbow grease and eventually got all the way to the American Hockey League. He has dressed in some preseason NHL games but not yet for a regular season game. Along the way, he has played against and dropped the gloves with some very tough men—maybe none bigger and tougher than Brian McGrattan. McGrattan is huge: 6'4" and 236 pounds. Alex is not huge: 6'0" and 180 pounds. Like his father, who never missed one of Brett's or Alex's games, he was often fighting much bigger men.

Alex has played mostly on the West Coast in his AHL career, Brett on the East. This meant that Pinky, back in PEI, could watch Brett play and then watch Alex play on TV. He did miss one night, which he regretted—the night his kid dropped the gloves with McGrattan. "It's a funny story. I only seem to remember Dad missing one game, even though it was on the West Coast."

The Gallants were out with friends on April 2, 2016, and the San Diego Gulls were in San Jose to take on the Barracuda, the AHL affiliate of the NHL's San Jose Sharks. When the game was over, Alex did what he always did, and called up his father. "I called him after I fought Brian McGrattan. Dad thought I was joking. To this day I think it was the one game Dad missed. I think he was pretty disappointed about that. Luckily, he found the video somewhere."

The video shows the fight but doesn't tell the whole story. McGrattan had 317 NHL games and 609 penalty minutes on his resume. Very few of those 609 minutes were for minor penalties. McGrattan was thirty-five, an established pro. Alex Gallant was twenty-three, an AHL rookie. McGrattan was a challenge and an opportunity for a young kid who had the fighting spirit of his old man. "I was having a great year with the fights. I was doing really well. Honestly for me, in that situation, it's a win-win for me no matter how I do, because it's Brian McGrattan, one of the best of all time. I have a lot of respect for Brian."

"I was actually trying to fight him all year. He kind of did the old 'naaa' thing and would skate away, just because he knew the anxiety that I had, going up against a guy like him. It wouldn't bother him [fighting me] because he was a legend, but I wanted to do it. But that one night the *Ice Guardians* were filming."

That's the film crew for the *Ice Guardians* documentary. The documentary, released in October 2016, was billed like this: "On-ice enforcers struggle to rise through the professional ranks of the world's most prestigious hockey league, only to be confronted with a newfound fight for the existence of the role itself." The film crew was in San Jose that night following McGrattan, onetime NHL enforcer now skating in the minors. Alex Gallant was about to get his wish. "My captain came up to me and said, 'The *Ice Guardians* are here filming. This might be the night that McGrattan might actually drop them.' I tell you, that's the most nervous I've ever been for a game. I had the cold towels going before the game. I was nervous for sure."

The nerves, the anxiety, the waiting. These things can take a toll on a player. Imagine stepping onto the ice, centre stage, in front of thousands of people, and engaging in a bare-knuckle fight. That can mess with a guy's mind. The nerves and anxiety can end careers. Alex fought through it; you have to wonder if Pinky went through the same thing when was pulling into the parking lot of the rink in Tignish during his playing days. "That's something I don't know. We never really talked about that. Like, 'Dad, were you nervous?' I don't know. I always remember him saying how he cut so easily and that would piss him off. That he didn't want to bleed because it almost looks like you lost. He hated how easy he cut. I don't know about the nerve thing. We never really talked about that too much, if he was nervous or not."

Alex and Pinky mostly just talked about technique and style.

Pinky was an excellent teacher: not a lot of defence, just a lot of punching. He told his sons to stick to throwing rights. "He thought we were good as righties. But I'd get bored, and I'd switch to left. And Dad would get mad at me when I'd go lefty. He'd say, 'You don't need to do that. Your right is strong enough. You can beat these guys with your rights.' But I'd be throwing rights and they'd tie me up, so I'd switch to left. I always knew when I was calling Dad after the games that if I switched to left, he was gonna have something to say about it."

Imagine, for a moment, being engaged in a fight with McGrattan, and worrying about which hand you are using. That's how much influence Pinky had on his boys. At any rate, Pinky missed this bout—live, anyway. It all started with the puck deep in the Barracuda's zone. Alex, on the left wing, took a pass from his defenceman, the classic breakout play. McGrattan and the puck met Gallant at about the same time. The big forward got Gallant with a solid check. Within about two seconds the gloves were off. Just like his brother Brett's first NHL fight, this one didn't last long, either—four seconds. Alex caught McGrattan with a right: "Gallant brought McGrattan to his knees in a hurry!" the play-by-play man screamed. In came the linesman and the fight was over.

"He was the best there was," says Alex. "And I wanted to go with the best there was at the time. I've got a lot of respect for Brian and that is something I wanted to do. I was doing well enough where I had the confidence in myself to do it. So that's what it was. He's a tough customer."

Alex won't say it, but he won the fight. Alex was, and is, a tough customer. He got that from his old man. His brothers did, too. He also got something else from Pinky. Alex is one of the most polite young men you will ever come across.

Soft-spoken like his father, the Gallants have the ability to change, almost transform, from off-ice nice guy to on-ice tough guy, and back again. "The way we play is intense but that's not us off the ice at all."

If he didn't already know it, Alex and his brothers got a chance to learn of the kindness of their father and the impact he had on the Island in the latter stage of Pinky's life.

In September 2015, Pinky Gallant—father, husband, agricultural salesman, former hockey player, hockey coach, and referee—was diagnosed with cancer. By 2018, he was heading to Moncton, New Brunswick, every three weeks for chemo and experimental immunotherapy treatment. Due to the side effects of the treatment, Pinky was forced to retire. The call went out on social media: "We would like to invite all of Mike's family, friends, customers, former teammates, and players that he coached over the past 50+ years to the Credit Union Place, on Friday, February 1st, for a benefit/auction and appreciation night to help this great community person."

They came from all over the Island for Pinky Gallant. Pinky was fighting but the end was getting closer. "You should have seen when they had the benefit," says Pinky's brother-in-law Mike. "The amount of people that showed up from Charlottetown that would've played against him, it was crazy. It was the biggest fundraiser ever in Summerside up until that point. The community showed up and raised $180,000 for Pinky. What does that say about the man? There were people at that benefit that Pinky would've known thirty years ago. It was huge. You couldn't get through the crowd."

It was right in the middle of the hockey season, but Alex was there, too. Alex was playing with the Chicago Wolves that season, the top farm team for the Vegas Golden Knights. At that time the Knights were coached by Pinky's old fan Gerard Gallant. "I think about this a lot," says Alex, "how lucky I was to have Turk in that organization because he's pretty close to my family. Turk was always checking in on how things were going with my dad. At the all-star break that year, I got a call from my coach, Rocky Thompson. He just said, 'Alex, you didn't really mention how your dad was doing. Turk just called and told us. I heard you're going home for all-star break. Let me be real clear: you're staying home.'"

It wasn't an easy decision for Alex to stay back in PEI once the all-star break was over, and he knew why. "That was hard for me because that would bother Dad so much. He didn't want us to miss games. He didn't want us home because of him and not being there for our team. But Rocky said Turk just called and said, 'You're staying home to get that time with your dad.' That was pretty special."

Alex got to spend a couple of months with his father. He was able to attend the benefit. "It was amazing, really, hearing what people thought of Dad, what a gentleman he was. The number of times I've heard that? The thing that people always say is Dad would stop to talk to everyone. Mom wouldn't mind me saying this, but it almost drove her nuts. She'd be in the truck waiting and waiting because Dad would stop to have a conversation with everyone. That's just the way he was. He was a gentleman. And after going through that, I know me and my brothers want to be the same way. I hope to be half the man he was. I want to be remembered the way my father was and take after him. It would be pretty special. I think that helps me try to be a good man off the ice, just like my father was."

After a couple of months at home, Alex went back to join

the Wolves on their run to the Calder Cup Finals. The Wolves lost the series to the Charlotte Checkers. Then Alex went back home. "It's almost like he was waiting for me to get home. About a month later he passed. We were all home. It was great to be all together and go through it as a family. It was so good to be home. I couldn't imagine being anywhere else."

Pinky passed away on July 17, 2019. He was sixty-one years old. He left behind his wife, his three sons, and his daughter, Jennifer. He left a lot of memories and a legacy on PEI. Every summer the Boys and Girls Club of Summerside holds their Celebrity Golf Tournament. It is a three-day adventure that attracts some of the biggest names in hockey and Canadian entertainment. If you stop by the Mill River Resort in O'Leary in late July, not far from where Pinky used to light it up on the ice, you might run into Pete Mahovlich, Denis Potvin, or Randy and Ricky from *Trailer Park Boys.* You'll always see Gerard Gallant. Turk's there every summer. You'll see Pinky's brother-in-law, Mike; he and Pinky used to play a lot of golf together. Billy MacKendrick is always around, and so are Brett and Alex. Usually, the eighteenth hole hosts the Gallant Brothers punch-out. You lightly tap your fist through a hole and a prize awaits. There's something new at the tournament these days: the Boys and Girls Club hands out the Mike "Pinky" Gallant Scholarship, which describes Pinky as a "fan favourite and legend in the 70s and 80s in PEI hockey, and there was no one tougher to lace up the skates than Mike 'Pinky' Gallant. The only thing bigger than his hockey grit was his enormous heart."

"Adam Binkley [Boys and Girls Club executive director] was a big part of the idea of a scholarship," says Alex. "He pushed for that. He thought a lot of my dad. Dad spent a lot of time at the

Boys and Girls Club growing up just down the street. It's a pretty special thing for Adam to help us work on."

In case you were wondering, no, Brett and Alex have never dropped the gloves. In fact, in their entire AHL careers, they have only played each other once. "I had Rocky Thompson as a coach that year. He talked to me before the game. He was quite clear. 'Absolutely no fighting your brother tonight,'" Alex recalls.

Thompson was no stranger to fights in hockey, and neither was his brother Jeremy; both were former pros. And just like Alex and Brett, only one, Rocky, made it to the NHL. But there was no need for Rocky to issue the warning: "Brett's my best friend. There's no way I would ever fight him. It just would not come to that. We're too close as a family and way too close as brothers."

Rocky did let Alex take the opening face-off. Brett was on the other side of the dot. "It was so special. We got to do the opening draw in my home barn. I never expected it. Brett slashed my stick and won the draw back. I slashed his stick to try to win it back. He was laughing the whole time we did it."

The older brother, the veteran, with the savvy move: a little hack to his brother's stick. How could a son of Pinky not be ready for that? "I didn't know it was coming. Some of the guys on my team who had played with Brett told me, 'I can't believe you didn't expect that. Come on.'"

That's about as nasty as things got on the ice that night. It was that rare Gallant phenomenon: a no-hitter.

They don't hit as much on the Island these days. There have been a few Senior teams recently, but nothing like the good ol' days that would have suited Brett and Alex quite well, just like it suited their father. "For sure, I would've loved to have played back then," says Alex. "Just hearing the old stories, Mom talks about it. On the weekend everyone packed the barn for Senior hockey or Junior hockey. That's what it was. It's just not even near that today, not even close."

Who knows? Maybe someday Pinky's boys will be back on the Island. Until then, Alex is going to take more of his father's advice and just keep playing. "He always told us, 'Play as long as you can.' He stopped to support us. He didn't regret that, but at the same time he regretted stopping playing. After he started coaching, he started playing again because he missed it so much. I just always remember him saying, 'Play as long as you can.'"

That explains why Alex and Brett are still slugging it out in the minors—not a figure of speech: in the 2021–22 season they combined for 213 penalty minutes, no mean feat in today's AHL. It also explains why someday you might see the Gallant boys

The Gallant boys out on the golf course. From
left to right: Brett, Pinky, Brad, and Alex.

back on the ice in PEI, turning a few heads, just like their father. "The Island tries to get the Senior hockey going but they just can't seem to make it happen. There's still a lot of talk with me and Brett. We talk about it with guys we played Junior with and still play with all the time [in the summer]. There's still a lot of talk that when we're all done, that maybe when we come home, we'll get a Summerside Senior team going. Who knows?"

CHAPTER 4

Oscar Gaudet

Moncton, New Brunswick

"The words *dipsy doodle dandy* might've been invented for Max Bentley," says Gair Maxwell. "But no one I have ever seen, and I mean this, in my entire life, personified it like the Big 'O'—Oscar Gaudet."

Gair Maxwell knows well of what he speaks. He called play-by-play for over 1,000 American Hockey League games throughout the 1980s and 1990s during his years as a sports reporter in Moncton, New Brunswick. And there is no player in Moncton lore that he holds in higher regard than Oscar Gaudet. "I can see it now. I can see the head fakes, the sudden shift in the moves. Even though he wasn't, as they say, fleet of foot, he had such control over the puck," he says. "And his vision was outstanding. We're talking the no-look pass all the time, and defenders had a hard time because Oscar was always in control of the play."

Gair grew up hearing of the legend of Oscar Gaudet, who grew up in a little town called Memramcook, about fifteen minutes outside of Moncton. His first chance to see Oscar in person was April 23, 1975, when he was just fourteen years old and one of thousands of fans jammed into the all-new Moncton Coliseum for game four of the 1975 Hardy Cup Finals.

The local heroes, the Moncton Bears, started the night with a 2–1 series lead over the Thompson Hawks in the best of five for the National Intermediate Senior Hockey Championship. "It was so packed. If the official capacity was 6,900, I am guessing there were probably 7,500 or so in the building. I'm sure they broke fire codes," Gair says. This was a time when there was no professional hockey in Moncton. The AHL finally showed up in 1978, but three years earlier the Senior Moncton Bears were a very big deal and Oscar Gaudet was the team's undisputed star. Gair adds, "The games were as intense as they were in the pros . . . guys were playing to win. Teams from Campbellton, Dalhousie, Saint John, Fredericton, Moncton. For us kids, this was the pinnacle, this highest level in our neck of the woods."

Moncton Coliseum was the biggest hockey stage in the province. Imagine a Senior hockey team, not a professional hockey team, selling out a 7,000-seat barn. That was Moncton in 1975. The city's hockey fans fell in love with the new Coliseum when it opened two years earlier. They didn't have much choice, really, as the town's former hockey cathedral, the Moncton Stadium, collapsed under the weight of a heavy snowfall during Christmas of 1970. Just like that, Moncton's most famous hockey barn disappeared—it was a tough lump of Christmas hockey coal for the city to swallow. But three years later the Coliseum was open for business, with the Bears installed as its main tenant. "The Coliseum was a jewel, brand spanking new," Gair says. "It was our version of Rogers Place in Edmonton right now, or the Scotiabank Arena [in Toronto]—fresh paint and brand-new, and that's where the Moncton Bears entered the picture."

The biggest Bear of them all, if not in stature, then at least in skill and hockey prowess, was Oscar Gaudet: by day a rep for Labatt Breweries, by night a hockey star, albeit a very humble one. Gaudet is a man of few words, preferring to do his talking on the ice. "We had a bunch of local guys and the owner of the team, Don Larin, he was the guy behind the scenes, and he brought in a couple of players from Quebec. We had a pretty good team year in '74, but we got beat out by Gatineau in Quebec. But everything came together with the '75 team. We made it happen," Oscar says, about the team that brought Moncton its first national hockey title in forty-one years. The Moncton Hawks won the Allan Cup in 1934. In 1975, Gaudet led the Moncton Bears to the Hardy Cup, the Canadian Intermediate A championship.

But here is what Oscar didn't tell me: he was the main ingredient, the true local legend, in the Bears' 1975 win. Heading into game one of the 1975 championship against the Thompson (Manitoba) Hawks, who had traveled all the way to Moncton for the series, the Bears had gone 16-1 in the playoffs. The stage was set for a best of five that kicked off on a Sunday night, 8:30 pm sharp, at the Coliseum. If the series went the distance, it would mean five games over five consecutive nights. At three bucks a ticket, the stadium was packed for game one. Just over four minutes into the second period, Oscar Gaudet made it 5–1 for the home side. It stood as the game winner. The Bears took game one, 5–4.

Game two was not even close: the Bears won 6–0. Gaudet didn't score a goal but set up four. Gerard McLaughlin wrote in the *Moncton Times Transcript*: "The Big O, Oscar Gaudet, dominated play almost every time he stepped on the ice." Oscar, as humble as ever, simply told the media after the game, "Our club is playing real good hockey. The win was a real team effort."

The stage was set for a sweep: all the Bears had to do was win their third game in three nights, but that did not happen. The Hawks played a wild game three. A stick fight broke out and many players left the benches to duke it out. Match penalties were assessed. It was a game straight out of *Slap Shot*. Moncton fans would have to wait at least one more night for a national title.

By the time Wednesday night's game four rolled around, it seemed as if the Big O was tired of waiting; he scored three goals to lead the Bears to a 4–1 win and a Hardy Cup title. A hat trick in the clinching game of the 1975 Hardy Cup! "I remember the last goal. It was the last minute of the game. They pulled the goalie, and I was able to get the puck out of the zone and shoot it from centre ice," Oscar remembers. That was the clincher for Moncton—an empty-netter with eleven seconds to go in the game. "Scoring goals is one thing but winning championships— that's the reason we play."

Allan Power played on Oscar's line the night the Bears won the Hardy Cup. He was just a young guy in his early twenties: "I was on the right side, a left-winger playing on the right side in that game with Oscar, with a young guy from Valleyfield, Quebec, by the name of Norm Piche." Allan, who went on to a career in hockey as a longtime NHL scout, saw nothing but magic from the thirty-three-year-old Labatt rep. "The goaltender and the defenceman couldn't handle Oscar's intelligence. Because as much as they tried to play him, they couldn't. The goaltender couldn't stop him because Oscar's eyes were on the blade of the stick. He was shooting from that angle. They didn't understand that. I had the best seat in the house, just flying right down that side."

"That was the magic of Oscar," says Allan. "I know this sounds strange, but he played like he had eyes in the blade of his stick. All the great shooters have it . . . it's something that can't be taught. They don't see their shooting angle from the eyes; they see it from their stick. Go stand behind your blade sometime—it will open a whole new world; holes in the net you've never seen before. Oscar never had to stand behind his blade to see those holes. He could see them from his eyes, about five feet and eight inches off the ice and the length of a stick away."

A natural passer, Oscar was always looking to set up a team-mate like Allan. But if the shot was the better play, Oscar would let it rip. "If he was in a better position to shoot, he did. That's rare even at the NHL level. I think that's rare today," says Allan.

For young fans in Moncton that night, Oscar Gaudet *was* the NHL. "This was the pinnacle—the Moncton Bears going to the Hardy Cup," says Maxwell. "All I remember is just being in the building. . . . I think they smoked cigarettes in the building back then . . . all I can picture is that big crowd and a haze of smoke."

Through that haze of smoke, the magician, the man they called the Big O, left the Coliseum that night a national cham-pion. The hat trick, the smoky stage—it sounds like rock star kind of stuff. But Oscar never acted like one, even in the dressing room after the championship win. "The quietness. The calmness of the pro that he was. There was no jumping up and down. There were no crazy celebrations. It was kind of . . . take a deep breath, we did it, that kind of thing," Allan says. "The composure of the pro while the rest of us young guys were just beside ourselves with excitement. I caught myself watching him and I thought, 'That's the way to behave.'"

Gaudet led the Bears with 60 points in the 19 playoff games he suited up for during the run to the Hardy Cup; 23 goals and 37 assists! He was the first star of game four. "The Big O, Oscar

Gaudet, the matchless Moncton puck wizard," wrote the report in the *Moncton Times Transcript,* "played the hockey game of his life Wednesday night, then put a lid on it."

Oscar was thirty-three years old, exhausted, and had just won a national title on home ice in front of his friends and family. In the jubilation of the dressing room, he took the time to reflect and then told the media, "I don't think I want to play anymore."

If this was it for Gaudet, what a way to finish! But saying *so long* to Moncton was nothing new, because the 1970s were Oscar's second act in town. Allan Power grew up during Act I: "As a young kid, nine, ten, eleven years old, I was one of those rink rats who lived close to the old Moncton Stadium. We'd go and watch Oscar's practices."

Those practices were with the Moncton Junior Hawks. He led the Junior Hawks with 30 regular season goals in 1961. That was the year they made it all the way to the Memorial Cup semifinal against St. Michael's College. Gaudet and the Hawks were no match for the Majors, but Gaudet did manage to beat their goalie, future Hall of Famer Gerry Cheevers, for a goal in the third and final game of the Majors' three-game sweep in Toronto.

"The National Hockey League or Major League Baseball or football, for us, was so far away we couldn't fathom what it was and what it wasn't," says Power. "So 'our' NHL players were guys like Oscar Gaudet who played for local Junior teams. Guys like Oscar were our Bobby Hulls and Stan Mikitas and Rocket Richards and all those guys. The awe of standing beside them was phenomenal as we were growing up."

If Allan timed it just right, he would arrive at church just in time to see his hockey hero, the guy who made it all the way to the 1961 Eastern Canada Memorial Cup Finals against the legendary St. Mike's College Majors, show up for Sunday Mass. "He'd get the big leather team jacket on. It wasn't because he wanted to be flashy. It was a sign that was phenomenally impressive outside of his hockey uniform."

Impressive both on and off the ice. When he was twenty-one years old, Oscar led the Moncton Beavers, who were playing in the Nova Scotia Senior Hockey League, with 56 goals and 74 assists for 130 points. Those points were good enough for second in league scoring. The NSSHL was littered with former and future pros, players like Simon Nolet, who went on to score 332 points in 562 NHL regular season games. He finished 22 points behind Oscar in the scoring race that year. After a couple more seasons of Senior hockey, including an astounding 182 points in his final season, Oscar's Moncton Act I came to an end. The pros came calling. "I got a call from Bob Wilson, a scout from Chicago. He came down and he brought me to training camp with Chicago. I made the team in Buffalo. I figured, I'm going to give it a shot," he says.

The Senior star, just twenty-three years old, left the only place he ever knew to see if he could make it all the way to the NHL during the "Original Six" era. His first stop was the Buffalo Bisons of the American Hockey League, the Blackhawks' top minor-league team. There was no shortage of future NHLers on that team. No problem. Oscar finished the season sixth on the team in scoring. "A lot of guys from the Maritimes or from this area, they go away but then they get lonesome and homesick. Before I left, I figured if I'm going, if I make the team, I'm staying," he says. "It was very rewarding to make the team in Buffalo. And then it was a piece of cake after that."

Oscar's professional career was off to a great start. The next season he ventured even farther from home. The Blackhawks shipped Gaudet to St. Louis. He finished second on the St. Louis Braves of the Central Professional Hockey League with 66 points, but he didn't get the call-up to Chicago. The Dallas Blackhawks were the next stop, and in his three seasons with the team, Oscar scored 213 points in 210 games, leading the team with 78 points in 71 games in 1969–70. Nobody in the league had more than his 53 assists, but he still didn't get the call-up to Chicago. All Oscar could do was watch as Chicago called his teammates up to the big club.

One of Oscar's teammates during his minor-league days was Dennis Hull, who played 40 games with St. Louis during Oscar's second pro season, splitting his time between the Braves and the Blackhawks in Chicago. On Oscar's induction page at the New Brunswick Sports Hall of Fame you'll find a quote from Dennis: "The greatest mistake Chicago ever made was trading Phil Esposito; its second greatest mistake was not putting Oscar in its regular centre lineup."

I called Dennis about that quotation. "That's a true story," he explains. "I thought he would have been perfect. The way he handled the puck. The way he skated. He would have been a perfect centreman for Bobby [Hull], who never had anybody to play with.

"I think they thought he was too slow, but Stan Mikita wasn't very fast, and he did okay. You don't have to be fast to play in the NHL and Oscar was smart. He could handle the puck and he could make wonderful passes. He always came to our training camp, and I was always disappointed when he didn't make the team.

"I didn't like it. I'm sure he liked it less. Sometimes the leadership isn't as smart as you might think they are."

Oscar figures he had his one true shot after the 1967 season.

The NHL was expanding to twelve teams for the 1967–68 season, and among the new teams was the St. Louis Blues. Oscar played in St. Louis during the 1966–67 season, and it was the perfect scenario: "I was supposed to get picked by the St. Louis Blues but what happened . . ."

The 1967 NHL Expansion Draft could not be any more different from the most recent NHL Expansion Drafts that we have seen. The Vegas Golden Knights were a juggernaut in their first NHL season. The Seattle Kraken found their stride by season two. The 1967 NHL Expansion Draft did not give the six new teams—the Blues, Minnesota North Stars, Oakland Seals, Philadelphia Flyers, Los Angeles Kings, and Pittsburgh Penguins—nearly as much top-notch talent to choose from, especially when you consider said talent had to be divided among six teams, and some more-than-quirky rules were involved in the draft.

For their expansion fee of $2 million per franchise, each new team got to select twenty players. The Original Six teams were not going to let their top players just walk. Each team protected one goalie and eleven skaters, and there were rules in place to keep young players and prospects exempt from the draft. Perhaps the biggest hurdle for the expansion teams, or for a guy like Oscar Gaudet looking to get a shot at the NHL and a decent payday, was that after a number of rounds, when a team lost a player in the draft, they could move another player they left unprotected, like Oscar, to their protected list. In short, when a team lost a player in the draft, they could add a player to their own protected list to make sure they didn't lose too many talented players. That is what happened to Oscar. He figured he would go to St. Louis, but when the Blues chose another player from Chicago, the Blackhawks then protected Oscar, and just like that he was out of the

Expansion Draft. He was not going to get a chance to play for the Blues. Instead, he would remain part of Chicago's very deep organization. "I fell into that situation," Oscar recalls all these years later, "and I didn't get drafted."

Oscar retired from the pros after spending the 1970–71 season with the Portland Buckaroos of the Western Hockey League. Naturally, he averaged almost a point per game: in 482 professional regular season games, Oscar accumulated 447 points. Incredible totals, but he never did get called up. Why? "I always ask myself that," he muses. "They had to say it was because of my speed and maybe that was true, but the Central League and the American League, back when I played, weren't much different from the NHL."

It was simply time to go home. Oscar had no intention of giving up on hockey, not by any stretch, but things were changing in life: "I retired because my oldest son, Rick, was starting school—that was the deciding factor."

Oscar took a job with Labatt and started playing Senior hockey again; Moncton Act II was under way. After just one season back home, things got a little interesting: in fall 1972, the world of professional hockey got a much-needed makeover with the arrival of the World Hockey Association (WHA). One of the WHA's founding teams, the Winnipeg Jets, signed Bobby Hull to hockey's first million-dollar contract. The Quebec Nordiques, another founding team looking for players that first season, wanted Oscar Gaudet, and they were offering serious money. But Oscar was no longer chasing big-league dreams: "It was a three-year contract that they offered but at the time I was retired. I had a good job, and the kids were in school. To leave everything and go back—I didn't see that being a good thing for the family."

So, Oscar stayed home. He played Senior hockey with some of the same guys he played with in Junior, and everything culminated that night in April 1975, when the Moncton Bears, led by the guy who almost made the NHL, came full circle back to Moncton to make a championship happen for his teammates and his fans: "To be honest, no, I never dreamed of it. It was just year to year but after seven years playing pro it was nice to come home, and, yeah, the Coliseum was a brand-new building."

For Allan Power, playing with Gaudet was also a full-circle moment. Really, how many of us get to grow up and play with our hockey heroes? I asked Allan, was it better to watch Oscar when he was ten years old, or play with Oscar when he was twenty? His answer: "You know, I can't say that one was better than the other. Through the eyes of a ten-year-old it was awe. As a twenty-year-old it was less awe, but more respect. Which one impacted me? Both did, in different ways. But I transferred the awe as a kid into respect [for Oscar] as an adult, which carries on to today."

Did Oscar really retire after that 1975 Hardy Cup win? Of course not. Oscar kept on playing Senior hockey. He won another Hardy Cup in 1979, the same season the New Brunswick Hawks of the AHL, the new big deal in town, were looking for a player. The team's head coach, longtime NHLer and future NHL head coach and front office executive Eddie Johnston, knew just who to call. "They had a lot of injuries, and I was still playing Senior. I was in good shape so EJ found me and asked me if I could step in," says Oscar. "I told him I'd play two home games and that was it and then I returned to my team—that's what happened."

The "old dipsy doodler" got an assist in one of the games. It was his first AHL point in fifteen years. "His skills were unbelievable. If you were to compare him to a player today, he'd be like Johnny Gaudreau or Daniel Brière," says Gair Maxwell.

"He had hockey sense that was unheard-of then, and maybe even now. Today's coaches and GMs see the game differently: they might have seen Oscar Gaudet for what he was—an offensive genius. *Incredible* puck sense. I bet he probably would've had a career in the NHL," adds Allan Power.

NHL or not, Oscar Gaudet is still a legend around Moncton, and still plays today. His playing weight back in the day used to swing between 170 and 175 pounds, and he currently tips the scales at 172. He still goes out to lots of Junior games. If he

Oscar Gaudet wearing the classic Black-hawks sweater during his days with the Original Six organization.

attends a Moncton Wildcats game at the Avenir Centre—the Coliseum isn't used for hockey anymore—Oscar can see his old number 11. A commemorative banner honouring the New Brunswick Sports Hall of Famer hangs for all to see. A Junior star, a Senior star, then a pro, only to come home and tear it up in the Senior ranks again . . . not bad at all. "Before I left for pro, I was younger and all excited about playing. Playing hockey was the main thing," Oscar says proudly. "Coming back . . . it was still fun; it was just really a sideline in a way. But winning in front of your home fans, winning the championship, that really took the cake."

CHAPTER 5

Keven Cloutier

Beauceville and Saint-Georges, Quebec

"**K**even Cloutier is a legend," says Sean McMorrow. Legend . . . that is a huge compliment. And it is coming from a huge guy. McMorrow, better known in hockey tough-guy circles as The Sheriff, is a well-known nuclear weapon in the hockey world. His pugilistic skills took him all the way to the NHL for one game with the Buffalo Sabres. He was also a feared fighter in the American Hockey League. And fear is what he struck into opponents in the Ligue Nord-Américaine de Hockey, better known as the LNAH. It is a Quebec-based league like no other. It evolved from the Quebec Senior AAA circuit in the early 2000s. The league made headlines for its punching power. McMorrow once fought a staggering 62 times in a single LNAH regular season. He is the exact opposite of Keven Cloutier. But there is a respect there, nonetheless.

"Sean's a legend, too," says Cloutier. "It's very touching to me to hear that. When you're a player, fans will say, 'This guy's good and he was one of the best in the league.' And it's nice to hear that. But when you hear a compliment like that from a player and the players you play against, it's even sweeter."

Cloutier never planned on playing pro hockey in the Saint-Georges region of Quebec. He never planned on playing pro hockey into his forties. He never planned on becoming the all-time leading scorer in the LNAH, but that is where his hockey career took him. "That's pretty awesome that he's still playing," says his old AAA Midget teammate Stéphane Veilleux, who went on to play 506 NHL regular season games, mostly with the Minnesota Wild. "It speaks volumes, really. He was always somebody that had a good work ethic, that always took hockey seriously. He was always working out in the gym and doing the best things that he could to get himself ready for hockey. I remember us playing in street hockey tournaments and he would be getting ready mentally and preparing himself to play random street hockey teams. That speaks to his competitiveness."

When they played AAA Midget together, Cloutier was his team's leading scorer with 77 points in 41 games. The team's second-leading scorer, Simon Gamache, made it all the way to the NHL. So did a couple of other players on the roster. Hockey had other plans for Cloutier. What's the difference between a player like Cloutier and a player like Veilleux who makes it all the way to the NHL?

"That's a difficult question to answer," says Veilleux. "Some of my teammates that were drafted higher or lower than me, that were considered better players, took different paths, for whatever reason. Some guys get chances. I played with some guys who did get chances and didn't take advantage of them. And there are also players that didn't get chances that were really good. There are a lot of different factors. And sometimes there's not always a reason that you didn't catch a break. Sometimes it's just the unknown. It's not an excuse, either, because there are players out there that did the work. They had the work ethic. They put in the time. They had the right character. Sometimes it just doesn't work out. That's life as well."

Keven Cloutier grew up in the town of Beauceville, Quebec. The town's claim to fame these days is that it is the home of the best women's player on the planet, Marie-Philip Poulin. It's a town of about five thousand, right beside the larger town of Saint-Georges. Beauceville is about an hour southeast of Quebec City. If you go back to Cloutier's formative years, Beauceville would likely fall under the category of Quebec Nordiques country. Future Hockey Hall of Famers like Peter Stastny and Michel Goulet played at Le Colisée, just up Highway 73 in Quebec City. But eight-year-old Cloutier didn't cheer for the Nordiques. He didn't really have a choice: "I know, I know, I should have been a Nordiques fan, but on my father's side of the family there were twenty-one kids, and they were all Canadiens fans, especially my grandmother. She would not accept us talking about the Nordiques. I did not hate the Nordiques, but I was a Canadiens fan because growing up, my father was taught that the Canadiens were the best. And I was kind of raised the same way."

Young Keven's favourite player was a tiny Swedish player known as Le Petit Viking. Mats Naslund was a 5'7", 160-pound scoring dynamo for the Canadiens. (At least, that's the height and weight that hockeydb.com lists for him.) Donning a strange Torspo helmet, Naslund was one of the Canadiens' steadiest scorers throughout the 1980s. He had a career high 110 regular season points for the Canadiens when they won the Stanley Cup in 1985–86. "He was a small, hardworking player. And in my league when I was young, I was kind of the shorter guy. So, I associated myself with Mats Naslund. He was a very skilled player, but not only skill, he would be working hard, and he was honest to the game. That's what I liked about him," says Cloutier.

Watching those Canadiens games, with his father, Leonandré, are some of the few memories Keven has of his dad. His father died in a car accident when Keven was only nine years old. His dad was always there for him, and went to Keven's games, but his memories of his father seemed to vanish after the accident.

"It's weird—I don't have many memories of my dad," says Cloutier. "He was there, but I don't know. It seems like everything blacked out for me a little bit. He was present. He was a hardworking man. He was doing a lot of hours at his job. He was always there for hockey, for me. He introduced me to hockey. He was a big fan, too. I saw pictures of me and him watching the Canadiens, just watching hockey games together."

Beauceville was like any other town in Quebec, or like every other town in Canada, for that matter. It was all hockey in the winter. Hockey took Keven to nearby Saint-Georges, where he could attend school and play hockey at the same time. Eventually his game took him far away from home. Like any other kid in the Quebec AAA Midget League, Keven wanted a shot at Major Junior hockey. In the 1997 QMJHL draft Keven was selected in the tenth round by the Rouyn-Noranda Huskies. That was a long way from home, at least a ten-hour drive. "It didn't matter to me. I wanted to play so badly in the Junior league that I was ready to go anywhere."

Things clicked with the Huskies. He did have to leave home, but so did hundreds (if not thousands) of other kids who wanted to make it to the NHL. He made the team full-time in fall 1998. He put up some solid numbers, too. But in his second full year in the league, Cloutier really took off. He finished second on the Huskies, with 91 points. We'll never know what he might have accomplished in a third year in Rouyn-Noranda because in summer 1999 Keven was traded from one end of the Quebec League to the other: he was now playing for the Cape Breton Screaming Eagles in Sydney, Nova Scotia.

He had heard complaints around the league from other players. The team was located too far away. Their closest road game was a four-and-a-half-hour bus ride to Halifax. It didn't matter; this kid would go anywhere to chase his hockey dream. "It really did not bother me. It was a new experience. I was ready to go there. They traded a good player for me. They wanted a veteran player who could perhaps be the leading scorer of the team. To be honest, I enjoyed the expectations. I liked it but I have to admit that I preferred playing in Rouyn-Noranda."

At any rate, he was off to Cape Breton. The Screaming Eagles wanted a points producer and Keven produced. He finished second on the team with 92 points. After that season, he turned twenty-one years old and his Junior career was over. The next step was the NHL, but he never got drafted: "I was expecting an NHL tryout. I didn't get it at that time. I had an agent but I'm not sure he was the right fit for me. He didn't have many players. He was a lawyer and doing agent stuff on the side. He only had one other client."

That agent got Keven a tryout with the American Hockey League's Worcester IceCats. They were the top farm team of the St. Louis Blues. Cloutier was off to Worcester, Massachusetts, where he would continue to chase the dream. But his stay did not last long: "I had a good camp, but I only played in one exhibition game with them."

After that game he got cut. It didn't matter that he scored a goal and added a couple of assists. Hockey is a business. The Blues had a lot of players under contract—players that the organization had drafted, invested money in, and promised to develop. Cloutier was just a free agent. A scout never put his neck out and said, "Sign this kid." Free agents are the easiest to send down or cut.

The IceCats sent Cloutier to Peoria of the East Coast Hockey League. They told Cloutier he'd impressed them and wished him good luck. If that's where he had to go to chase his hockey dream, so be it. Things did not start well, though: "The coach told me when I got there that I had to prove him wrong. He said that he did not have good experiences with French guys. I said, 'Okay, I'm just going to do what I do. I'll work hard and see what happens.'"

Cloutier got third- or fourth-line duty. That's the way it goes in the minors, if you were not drafted or under contract with the big club. Hundreds of minor-league players have to cope with this reality every year. "It's really, really tough [not being under contract to the NHL team]. Maybe when you have a good agent working for you, who was known in the business of hockey, maybe the guy can work for you. But I was alone. I was doing my best. It was very tough when I was in Peoria. I would see kids arriving from the NCAA and they would have a contract. The team would play them in front of me because of the contract that they had. I remember thinking, 'Man, if I had that chance I would produce.' If you're not drafted, if you don't have a contract and you're a free agent in the East Coast League, it is very tough to make a name for yourself."

When you're on the third or fourth line you're not getting power play time. You're not getting offensive chances. For Cloutier, a scorer by nature, this meant fewer opportunities to prove himself. Off the ice he was living with a roommate he didn't really know. Things were not working out as he thought they would.

Right after Christmas, the kid who would go anywhere to chase his dream wanted to go home. In January, he made a call to the general manager of the Saint-Georges-de-Beauce Garaga of the Quebec AAA Senior League. "I said, 'Hey, do you have a spot for me? I just wanna come back. I'm having a hard time here. I'm not happy. I just don't like it here. I don't even feel like playing hockey anymore.' And he said, 'You called me three days too late. They have a rule that after January 5 you cannot sign any free agent players.'"

There was no going home for Cloutier. He was stuck, deep down the depth chart of an ECHL team, and his love of the game, something he had always had, was nowhere to be found. He finished his first pro season with 15 goals and 26 assists for 41 points. "I know that doesn't sound like much, but believe me, given my ice time, those are enormous offensive numbers."

When the season ended, Cloutier met with Peoria's general manager. He admitted that he had not gained the trust of the coach. He told the team that if they did not move him, he would not be coming back to Peoria. That off-season he was traded to the Pensacola Ice Pilots. His chase of the dream was now taking him to Florida: "I told myself, the dream is to play in the NHL. I've got to make the most of it."

Things were better in Pensacola, but something was still off. Cloutier was still a guy without a contract. He finished his second pro hockey season with numbers almost identical to his first. He scored 14 goals and added 31 assists for 45 points in 69 regular season games. "I just felt like the East Coast League wasn't a good match for me. The traveling was tough. I did have a better year and I played a little more. I was more on the third line instead of the fourth. It was okay, but I did not enjoy it a lot."

Cloutier's ECHL experience was over. "Those were probably my two toughest years in hockey." He decided to go home. But how long would he hang around?

Cloutier asked the Saint-Georges team for a spot on their Senior team. Done. The team also hooked him up with a job: he began his career as a 911 dispatcher. But the NHL now seemed so far away. He was a semipro hockey player with a day job. Something came back, though, as soon as he joined his local Senior AAA team in the fall of 2003.

"It didn't take long before I found the love of the game again in Saint-Georges. They were always the best team in the league for many years. I just kind of jumped onto the team and there were a lot of veterans, and the guys were just awesome to accept me. I made a lot of friends. There were a lot of local players back in those days. We had at least ten or twelve guys from Beauce. I knew a lot of them. It was awesome. That's why I probably started performing quickly in this league, because of how the team accepted me and the chemistry we had."

Cloutier's love of the game was back. He had traveled all over the United States for two years in the minor leagues chasing the NHL dream, and it had cost him. With his renewed spirits, he was second on his team that season with 75 points in 46 games. He played on a line with Sabres draft pick Philippe Audet and a longtime pro named Trevor Jobe: "We had very, very good players. We were better than an East Coast team."

Their team hosted the Allan Cup during that first year. They had lost out in their league playoffs in a game seven double-OT loss but got an automatic spot in the Allan Cup as the hosts. Armed with several ex-NHLers, including their goaltender, Jean-François "JF" Labbé, who had played for Columbus in the NHL the previous season, Saint-Georges cruised through the Allan Cup. The team outscored its opponents 30–10 and went undefeated to win the Canadian Senior Hockey Championship. "It was fun winning that together and everything, but I think we were too good for the tournament," Cloutier says with a chuckle.

Cloutier was a skilled guy in the AAA Quebec Senior Major Hockey League. Skill was one side of the league's equation. The other side was toughness. Not "slam you into the boards" toughness, but "two dudes taking off their helmets and squaring off at centre ice." Each team in the league was loaded with tough guys. Games were filled with scraps. There could be three or four per game, sometimes more. (As far as Cloutier can recall, there was no Lady Byng Trophy in the QSMHL.) Toughness and skill sold in the Quebec Senior circuit. Guys like Keven provided the skill. Guys like Sean McMorrow or Joël Thériault provided the fisticuffs. "It didn't matter to me. I knew that in this league there were a lot of fights but most of the fights are between the tough guys. They are there to do a job. Good players, they can play. Of course there's intimidation but it didn't matter to me because in Saint-Georges we had a good team and great chemistry with the guys. The tough guys would take care of things if anything happened. It was not a factor for me."

"I've seen a lot of crazy things [in this league]. So many, many brawls. We had one, one day in Saint-Georges on a Sunday night. Oh, it was crazy. So many things happened. We were playing the toughest team in the league. Two of our tough guys were suspended and the other one was injured. Let's just say we paid a price that night."

Cloutier could take the abuse. The one barn in the LNAH where you do not fool around is the Colisée de Laval. It is a

3,500-seat madhouse, a classic old hockey barn. (It is literally a barn, with the curved roof.) The rink was and is famous for its frothing-at-the-mouth, fight-loving fans. Cloutier got a taste of what it was like in "The House of Pain" early in his days with Saint-Georges. Laval was armed to the gills with players like Patrick Côté and Mike Bajurny. Those are LNAH names that would send a chill up the spine of any player in the league. With the Garaga up 2–1 late in the game, Laval pulled their goaltender to go with a six-on-five attack to try to tie up the game. Saint-Georges's plan was, of course, to hold the lead and with any luck, add an empty-netter. This, Cloutier soon found out, was not the type of place where you try to pad your stats with an empty-net goal. An empty-netter, the veterans knew, would mean immediate pain for the visitors.

Laval called a time-out. There was a minute to go. Cloutier and his teammates headed to their bench for a pep talk from the coach. Cloutier was expecting strategy, breakouts, X's and O's. The coach didn't say a word. Instead, one of the veterans spoke up. He did not give a pep talk—he issued a stern warning. "He was quite clear. He said, 'I don't want one guy scoring in that empty net. If you do, you're by yourself. I don't give a shit. If you get the puck, shoot it in their corner. Just let it die in the corner. And we don't want an offside late because they will put their tough guys on the ice. We will get beat up.' I thought, 'Holy shit!' We had one or two [tough] guys on our team, that was it. We could not match them. I remember thinking, 'Don't score on the empty net.'"

Good thinking. Saint-Georges survived that night relatively unscathed. It helps that Cloutier didn't really need another empty-netter. He has scored hundreds of goals in his LNAH career. He is the league's all-time leading scorer. Aside from a couple of stints in Switzerland, he has always played at home, for the team now known as the Saint-Georges Cool FM 103.5. He has seen his league go from absolute mayhem on ice to a slightly more reserved style of play. *Slightly.*

"I think he was one of those guys," says Sean McMorrow, "even through at the time the LNAH was just known as a fighting league, where there might only be one good line, Keven was always the best player. And we always kept the hope that the league could continue to have skill players because Keven Cloutier is here, you know what I mean? If Keven Cloutier plays here, then this guy could play here, too. I think the league would even use him to recruit other good players during that time when it was almost two or three lines of just tough guys." Maybe this is why McMorrow would share a wink and a nod of respect with Cloutier every time they played against one another.

Cloutier is now approaching 1,000 points in the league. The numbers, he tells me during our conversation, do not really matter to him. Here's what does: if he didn't make the move back home close to twenty years ago, when he lost his love of the game, there's no chance he'd still be getting paid to play the game he loves, let alone get to play it in the place he grew up. "As a hockey player, when you lose the love of the game, it's so hard just going to the rink. You kind of pout. You don't feel like going and it is hard to perform. But at Saint-Georges, I was very happy here from the first day. I felt like I was in the right place. I just felt like I was in the right place at the right moment."

Cloutier's hockey home was the home he always had. It was the home he had to leave to chase his NHL dream. That dream didn't work, but hockey takes different players on different paths. Cloutier is still playing in front of people he grew up with, and people he has known for his entire life. It was not his initial hockey dream, but it means a lot to him now. "I always tried to play for Saint-Georges. Sometimes the guys on the team—if they were not from Saint-Georges, they'd say, 'Hey, it's okay if we lose.' But they're not playing in front of people that they cross paths with at the supermarket. That really helped me to perform. Just to be playing in front of my people, I'm very thankful for that. I still enjoy playing in front of the crowd in Saint-Georges. I think they're the best fans in hockey.

"I would've loved to have played at a higher level. I feel that maybe the timing was off for that. I know I could've at least played in the American Hockey League. Maybe I could have had a career there. But hey, that's how it happened for me and I'm fine with it. I am at peace."

At peace that he is at home, playing the game he loves, in front of the people he loves. The same people who love him.

Keven Cloutier is presented with a puck and plaque, by Cool FM chairman Stephane Rouleau, to commemorate his LNAH record-setting 329th career goal. No one has scored more goals in LNAH history than Keven.

CHAPTER 6

Rob McGonigal

Arnprior, Ontario

Arnprior, a town of about eight thousand in the Ottawa Valley, sixty-five kilometres from Canada's capital, is like a lot of small Canadian towns. Throughout history, when the call came to serve, it sent its best to fight. Seventy-six young men from Arnprior fought in World War I and eighty-four more fought for Canada's effort in World War II.

For years afterward, whenever the local Royal Canadian Legion held an event to pay tribute to those who fought, a local businessman named John McGonigal would always step up with others to help out. McGonigal served in the reserves during World War II, and although he never ended up going to Europe, he never forgot those who did. Every year McGonigal, who owned Arnprior TV Centre at 90 John Street North, would provide speakers or TVs for the Legion's events, free of charge. "He would just let them borrow them and they'd bring them back. The idea of being humble, that was a big thing for my grandfather," says Sean McGonigal.

Sean, a teacher, is one of the seventh generation of McGonigals to call Arnprior home. His grandfather John raised his family in town. John and his wife, Kay, had a son named Robert and, later on, a daughter named Erin. Robert—Sean's uncle—was a pretty good hockey player. "He [Rob] was a very humble person when it came to his hockey career. You would have to ask him about it. He wouldn't go out of his way to tell you, 'Oh, yeah, I did this,' or, 'I did that.' He kind of gets forgotten in Arnprior."

Rob (or Robbie) McGonigal grew up playing his minor hockey both in his hometown and throughout the Ottawa Valley. "I remember Robbie through minor hockey," says Warnie Richardson, a retired Nipissing University professor. "We had a loop in the Ottawa Valley. There was Shawville, there was Renfrew, there was Arnprior, there was West Carleton, there was Barry's Bay, Pembroke, and Eganville. And we all played in a league together, so we saw one another quite a lot over the life of a minor hockey career. Each team has certain players that stand out: with Arnprior it was Robbie. From as long back as I can remember, including Atom and Peewee, Robbie was kind of the Arnprior star. He was quite talented."

A few years later Robbie was talented enough to get a chance to play outside of Arnprior and the Ottawa Valley loop. Robbie hit the road and headed a couple of hours east to try to make an impression on the Cornwall Royals. Close to the Quebec border on the far eastern side of Ontario, Cornwall had a team in the Quebec Major Junior Hockey League. The ten-team league was full of high-flyers like future NHLers Lucien DeBlois and Mike Bossy. Bossy would end up second in the league that season with 79 goals. Cornwall's head coach was Orval Tessier. He had played 59 regular season games in the NHL's Original Six era. A few years down the road, he would become the head coach of the Chicago Blackhawks. Robbie McGonigal stuck around for seven games.

According to family lore, passed down from John to his grandson Sean, an injury and Robbie's lack of desire to adopt a certain style of play popular at the time cost him his spot on the Royals. The word *goon* is thrown around a lot when you talk about hockey in the late 1970s. There's a reason for that: hockey was loaded with them at the time. Goon, tough guy, enforcer, whatever you want to call it, the role of that player was to drop the gloves and fight. Sometimes, at least it would appear to some observers, for nothing at all. It was a role Robbie did not want to take on.

"At sixteen, he broke his collarbone," says Sean. "They told him that they would keep him, but they wanted him to become the full-time goon for them once he got healthy. And at sixteen years old he was like 150 or 140 pounds. He said to them, 'I can offer more than just being a goon. I have skill as well.'"

The Royals did not take Robbie up on his offer. He was out of Cornwall. A sixteen-year-old kid without a hockey home.

Enter Rockland, Ontario. It was not Major Junior hockey, but hey, it was closer to home, an hour or so from Arnprior, just across the river from Thurso, Quebec, the home of Guy Lafleur. Rockland was not a big city. Far from it. It was a town of only four thousand and home to the Rockland Nationals, a third-year team playing in a brand-new building in the Central Junior Hockey League, a Tier II Junior A loop made up of teams surrounding Ottawa. It was a big-budget team owned by several businesses. The owners were in business for one thing—to win. So far, they had not. The team lost a combined $30,000 in its first two years of operation. Year three would be a little different. The team would still lose money, but this time they'd win—everything.

The man in charge of putting the Nationals together on the ice was the team's thirty-three-year-old general manager and head coach, Bryan Murray. The future NHL head coach and general manager from Shawville, Quebec, was an Ottawa Valley guy, too, like Robbie. In the spring of 1976, Murray, Robbie McGonigal, and the Rockland Nationals won the Centennial Cup—the Canadian Junior A championship. According to Warnie Richardson, Robbie, who was still just a kid, made an impression on Murray that would last a lifetime. "I was talking to Bryan Murray when he was in Ottawa. . . . He was always saying that he needed a defenceman like Robbie McGonigal who could rag the puck out of his own end when you were in trouble. I remember that distinctly, Bryan saying he was looking for players like Robbie, because he could rag the puck like crazy."

After that national championship season with Rockland, Murray pulled Robbie with him to Pembroke, Ontario. The owners in Rockland had sold the team, and Murray took a job with another team in the Central League, the Pembroke Lumber Kings, a team Robbie would eventually captain. That's where he would suit up with his old minor hockey foe, Warnie Richardson. The two would become teammates and, after their days in Pembroke, lifelong friends. That first year in Pembroke, Warnie got to see his new buddy's magic up close: "Robbie was a fantastic hockey player. He was among the best open-ice hitters. Robbie was not dirty at all. Now, having said that, you didn't linger in front of the net around Robbie McGonigal, or you'd be on your arse. He would catch you with your head down. He was very good at catching someone in the open ice and hitting them very, very hard." Warnie laughs as he thinks of his old buddy, laying the body on an unsuspecting forward. "He would do tremendous damage in the open ice but, again, he was never dirty."

Pembroke was almost the perfect on-ice home for Robbie.

Sitting right on the Ottawa River, it is known as the "Heart of the Ottawa Valley." It wasn't too far from Arnprior as well, about forty-five minutes northwest up the Trans-Canada Highway. In the mid-1970s around 15,000 people called Pembroke home. The Junior A Lumber Kings had been around town since 1961. The Lumber Kings played their home games in the Pembroke Memorial Centre, which had opened ten years before. The official opening of the building was an exhibition game between the Pembroke Senior Lumber Kings and the Montreal Canadiens. Twenty-five years later it was not unusual to see more than 2,200 fans jammed into the barn to watch the Junior Lumber Kings. "The fans were very boisterous, very supportive," Robbie's sister, Erin, says with a laugh. "The place was always packed. It was an older arena. It was not a new modern facility by any stretch of the imagination. It was a great place to play hockey. I made a lot of friends myself there."

So did Robbie and his teammates. Pembroke was the type of community where people wouldn't just cook for the local hockey players and drop off the food; they would invite the players right into their homes. "There was one lady there, Grace Brophy—she always had all the boys back to her home to have meals after all the home games. There was just something about the community there that was very supportive of their team," Erin recalls.

Maybe it was Grace's cooking. Maybe it was Bryan Murray's coaching. Whatever it was, the Lumber Kings went on a tear during the 1976–77 season, rolling their way through the Central Junior League to win the league championship. They took out Nepean four games to two to win the league title in late March 1977. Robbie was after his second straight Centennial Cup title. Next up for the Lumber Kings was a best of seven against La

Tuque, the champions from the Quebec Ice Hockey Federation. The series started in the small Quebec town, hostile territory in those days. "Robbie hit someone. I can't remember the player, but it was early in the series. He hit someone in their building and the building went quiet."

There is nothing quite like sending a chill through a building, especially on the road. That home crowd advantage had been immediately taken away from La Tuque. A group of Pembroke fans had planned to fly to La Tuque for the series, but a snowstorm made quick work of their plans. Noise or not, McGonigal had set the tone. "In those days when you go into those kinds of buildings, two things would happen. You'd get a good lead, or your heavyweight would go against their heavyweight. And if your heavyweight won [the fight] it deflated the building. And a big hit could also do that. And Robbie would do that. Many times, it would be a big hit early in the series."

McGonigal set the tone, not with a goal, not with a fight, but with a body check. The Lumber Kings took the first two games of the series by a combined score of 15–7, then swept the series. The Lumber Kings then took out the North York Rangers four games to two. Next up, a sweep of the Charlottetown Generals. With that, the Lumber Kings were off to Prince Albert, Saskatchewan, for a best of seven for the Centennial Cup. A second straight Centennial Cup for Robbie McGonigal was just four wins away. But it was not meant to be: the Prince Albert Raiders won the Centennial Cup in four straight games. As usual, Robbie's stats didn't jump out during the series. He was that kind of player; the guy whose name isn't always mentioned in the postgame summary sheet. But his coaches knew. His teammates knew. "He killed penalties," says Warnie. "He was great at killing penalties. The statistics don't do him justice that way. I can tell you this, if it was a power play or if it was or a clutch penalty kill, he'd be on the ice. Guaranteed."

Robbie was one of three Lumber Kings selected to the tournament all-star team by journalists and broadcasters covering the series. Six hours after losing game four by a score of 4–3, the Lumber Kings boarded a bus to Saskatoon to catch a flight to Ottawa.

McGonigal was named the captain of the Lumber Kings for the next season. Pembroke won another league title in 1978. That was three Junior A league crowns for Robbie in three years. Murray ended up leaving the Lumber Kings after 1978. In fact, three years later, he was coaching in the NHL with the Washington Capitals. A lot of Robbie's teammates were moving on to university hockey in the United States or Canada, such as Warnie Richardson, who ended up playing at Acadia University: "Most of us knew that we weren't going to make a great deal of money out of hockey. It wasn't going to be a career but if we could get our schooling out of it that's what we were trying to do . . . that's how I ended up at Acadia."

Robbie had offers to play university hockey, but he was not interested. "All he ever wanted to do was go back to the Ottawa Valley and start a business. That was his thing," recalls Warnie.

Robbie was a Valley guy. Robbie was an Arnprior guy. And just like his dad, he wanted to own his own business in his hometown. Robbie went back home and set his sights on the masonry business. He had an apprenticeship at home before he moved out west to finish things up in Calgary, then moved back to Arnprior to start his second life as a businessman. "My grandparents helped him start the company," says his nephew, Sean. "He started it in Arnprior and did jobs all over the Valley."

The company started small. It ended up doing very well. Robbie McGonigal the hockey player was now Rob McGonigal the businessman. McGonigal Construction became a mainstay in the Valley. What made him successful on the ice perhaps helped him in business. According to his sister, Erin, "Robbie was very tenacious at times. When people would tell him he wasn't good enough, he wanted to show that he was, if that makes sense.

"He also had a very gregarious personality. A lot of people liked him. He was always very friendly. He would never walk by somebody and not speak to them if he knew them. He was always a bit of a jokester. It would be nothing for you to be on the other side of the street and him to yell over at you. He had that kind of bigger personality to him."

The old minor hockey star was now a big businessman in his little town. "He was just a fixture. He was so well-known in the Ottawa Valley and so respected as a hockey player, and then just as a human being in Arnprior. But then as a businessman I started to hear good things about him as well," says Warnie.

Warnie is not talking about the dollars and cents of being a businessman. He is talking about giving back. Just like his dad, John, Robbie gave back. Much of his charity work was for the local kids at the rink, although he never really wanted anyone to know about it. If a kid couldn't afford minor hockey registration, Robbie would step in and take care of the costs. Or if a team wanted to order a set of hoodies, they would somehow show up, free of charge. Sean saw it up close when he was coached by his uncle early in his minor hockey days: "He would do it very quietly. He didn't need his name to be publicized; the other companies in town made sure you knew that they donated the money for this kid to play. My uncle was always a very silent partner in that sense."

"He did pay hockey fees," says his sister. "He sponsored tournaments. He was very invested in things like that. And he wanted it kept quiet. Why? I don't know. I think he wanted to keep the focus more on the kids. He was in it for the love of the game, and he wanted all the kids to have the ability to enjoy the game. It wasn't about him. He didn't want his picture in the paper."

Sean became a teacher. He went to Nipissing University, where one of his professors was Warnie Richardson. Robbie and Warnie never lost touch. "Long after hockey was over, Robbie was genuinely interested in what you were doing with your life, with how your family was doing, how your mom and dad were doing. You wouldn't go for a very long stretch without him touching base and checking in with you."

Robbie didn't have to go too far to check in with his old Junior coach: in the summer of 2004, Bryan Murray was named the head coach of the Ottawa Senators. Robbie was a Sens season ticket holder; in fact, his seats weren't too far from the coach's wife. "Geri sat not too far behind Robbie," begins Erin. "He would laugh at her. Robbie was known to be a bit of a jokester. She would always read a book during the games because it was too stressful for her to watch the games. Robbie looked at her one time and said, 'Mrs. Murray—you need to turn the book the right side up so you can actually read it.' That's how he joked around."

Nephew Sean says Robbie would let Bryan have it, too: "He had a great sense of humour. When Bryan Murray got honoured in Shawville, Robbie was at the ceremony. Now I don't know what Murray said [onstage] but my uncle made some smart-ass comment. Murray picked him out of the crowd—he was up onstage—and he said, 'McGonigal, is that you?'"

Robbie's business was thriving. He did what a lot of guys do: he fell in love and got married. He and Janet raised two kids, Lauren and Tim.

Then the unexpected happened. Rob was diagnosed with melanoma. Initially, his doctors thought Rob was in for a long fight: "They told him that he would have twelve years to live," says Sean.

But six weeks after he was diagnosed with melanoma, Robert McGonigal passed away with his family by his side. He was fifty-six years old.

"He was an Ottawa Valley guy," says Warnie. "We saw ourselves as being somewhat brothers because we were from that small geographic location."

"He was very much a leader. He was very protective of his teammates. He was something to watch," says Erin. "When he would talk about it [hockey], he'd talk more about the friendships he had—the boys. He was still in touch with Warnie. He was still in touch with Dave Jackson and the Nixon brothers. I could go down the team list."

It was the kindness, the selflessness, the stepping up to help with costs for a kid he might not have even known, that speaks to who Robbie was. Or as Erin tells me: "That was his essence."

"We have a long family history here," she says. "We lived in different places but we both gravitated back here. We both appreciated what it was. I think it was very important for him, he wanted his kids to grow up here. He wanted them to have the small-town life.

"He definitely left a big hole. I don't know [who can fill it] . . . I shouldn't say it like that. There have been a few people who have passed away who were very community-minded. It will be interesting to see who will take their place.

"I think he was admired a lot by a lot of people, but I don't think he knew how much."

Rob McGonigal, in a rare photo, during
his time with the Lumber Kings.

CHAPTER 7

Dave Tucker

Cambridge, Ontario

In spring 1999, Kevin Tucker was wrapping up his first professional hockey season. He was not playing under the bright lights
of the NHL. He was not playing just a step away from the Show,
in the American Hockey League. He was buried deep in the minors, toiling for the Saginaw Gears of the United Hockey League.

"They called it the Cocktail League," says Tucker. "The United
League was kind of high pay for high entertainment value. The
fans weren't there to watch hockey. They were there to watch the
fights and the scraps."

Tucker had come to the UHL after three years at Acadia University in Wolfville, Nova Scotia. In Canadian university hockey
there was no fighting at all. Even if there was, Kevin wasn't there
to do that anyway; he was at Acadia to score. That's what he did
on all his hockey stops, from his beginnings in Junior and then on
to Notre Dame College in Wilcox, Saskatchewan. During his final
year at Acadia, Kevin led the Axemen in scoring with 32 points in
26 games. After three years at Acadia, Kevin joined the Canadian
National Program. All was going according to plan, but then he
got cut. That's when he decided to turn pro: it was something

his father, Dave Tucker, always told him to do if he ever got the chance: "All he ever said to me was if you get the opportunity to go pro you make sure you do it—I don't care where, just do it, or you will regret it."

Now, a few months after signing his first pro contract, here was Kevin Tucker playing for the Saginaw Gears. He had started his professional career with the UHL's Winston-Salem Icehawks, but his time in the Carolinas only lasted thirty-five games. One of his teammates in Winston-Salem was a guy named Johnny Nelson. They knew each other from college hockey. When Tucker was playing for Acadia, Nelson was playing for the University of Prince Edward Island: "We were thick as thieves. We pretty much forced the trade to Saginaw."

How can players at this level force a trade? In the big leagues, players can hold out for millions, forcing the hand of owners and GMs. But in the lower levels of minor-league hockey? "We were not doing what our coach asked of us in terms of off-ice activities," Tucker says with a chuckle. "We were having a good time."

Tucker and Nelson took their talents to Saginaw, Michigan, but the Gears finished dead last in the eleven-team UHL. It didn't help the team's cause that their owner also owned another team in the league, the Flint Generals. In fact, the owner had traded many of the Gears' best players to the Generals, in the hope that the Generals could go on a decent playoff run. That didn't sit too well with the guys left on the Saginaw roster. Which brings us to a late–March 1999 matchup between the Generals and the Gears.

"As players we were all pissed-off," says Tucker. "At one point in that game we were on the power play. I had the puck behind our net. Johnny came skating by to go behind the net. He took the puck from me and then he said, 'Watch this.'"

Tucker didn't know what was coming. He had seen quite a few things in his first professional season in the UHL: fights in the stands and plenty of suspensions. One night his team's Zamboni driver had to play goalie for them, and the guy still flooded the ice in between periods. But he had never witnessed what Nelson was about to do, seconds after he picked up that puck on a Saginaw power play and flew up the ice: "He stopped at centre ice and pointed at the Flint bench. Then he took a slapshot at their coach's head."

That is how you start a bench brawl. "Both benches cleared. There were fans on the ice. There were players in the stands. It went on for a couple of hours. There were arrests. All kinds of stuff."

In the middle of it all was twenty-four-year-old first-year pro Kevin Tucker, perhaps wondering why he listened to his father, Dave. And Dave Tucker knew something about the subject: years before, he had the chance to go pro, but he never went. Something he would regret.

John Herbert has seen a lot of hockey. His career as a newspaper writer gave him an up-close look at some of the game's best. It's a view most hockey fans could not help but envy. Before the World Junior Championship tournament was a national Canadian event every Christmas, it flew under the radar. It was so small, in fact, that when Canada won the World Junior Championship in 1982, the tiny rink in Rochester, Minnesota, didn't even have a recording of the Canadian national anthem to play. The players, such as future NHLers Scott Arniel, Paul Boutilier, Garth Butcher, and Randy Moller, loudly sang the song themselves. Herbert was there: "It was a Sunday-afternoon game against the Czechs. Some media guys parachuted in, like [Al] Strachan and a couple CBC guys. I went up with Strachan and a couple of guys by car. We rented a car, but I didn't tell them I was coming back on the Team Canada bus, because I figured that would be the best story angle. Times have changed. I helped carry cases of beer onto the bus on the way home."

A few years before that, Herbert was one of the few media members covering the 1978 World Juniors. The games in Quebec City got decent crowds, but hardly anyone went to watch Team Canada (adorned in a strange blue maple leaf uniform) play when Montreal hosted games in the historic Forum: "I was the only media guy there. It was over Christmas. I think I was the only fan there, too. There might've been three hundred fans a game at the Forum. It seemed liked that—maybe five hundred, tops. There was hardly anybody there."

That means hardly anyone witnessed a sixteen-year-old Wayne Gretzky score 17 points (in six games) for Canada in that tournament. But Herbert did, and he knew Gretzky well. He was covering him that same winter in Ontario. Herbert was an Ontario sports reporter when Gretzky was playing for the Sault Ste. Marie Greyhounds. In his only season in the Ontario Hockey League (OHL), seventeen-year-old Gretzky led the league with 182 points in 64 games. "I covered Gretzky from Junior B. I gave him his nickname. Did you know that? I called him 'The Great One,'" laughs Herbert. "Yeah, that's a story. He was playing for Sault Ste. Marie. There was a game in London one night and he got five points. I was covering it. Of course, the headline on my story said, 'The Great Gretzky.' I didn't write that—it wasn't what was in the story—but ever since then he's always blamed me for the name. To this day. And this was forty years ago!"

Herbert saw Darryl Sittler play Junior hockey. He saw Dino

Ciccarelli play Junior hockey. Before he was a reporter, Herbert was just a kid growing up in Cambridge, Ontario. He would sneak into the legendary Galt Arena Gardens just to get on the ice early. He has been around hockey for as long as he can remember. He's been around the Great One for more than forty years, but there's still one name that has a place in his mind: Dave Tucker. The same Dave Tucker who told his son, Kevin, that if he ever got a chance to play professional hockey, take it.

"As a kid, maybe I was mesmerized a little bit by Dave," says Herbert. "He was such a great player. I always thought everybody knows somebody who should've made it, and everybody knows somebody who didn't make it. And that's kind of the way I look at Dave. He was good. Really, really good. Everywhere he went he was successful. He started out in minor hockey in the Galt system. He was the captain and the leading scorer and the dominant player. Then he went to Hespeler."

The Galt Arena is, in a word, beautiful. It is also historic. There is not a hockey rink on the planet that has been around longer than Galt Arena Gardens. From the outside, it looks like a mini Maple Leaf Gardens. It was built in 1921 and since then has been completely renovated, but I swear, if you close your eyes, you can picture Gordie Howe cutting through the ice. Because at one time he did. Or maybe Bobby Hull or Terry Sawchuk or Howie Meeker. They played there, too. So did Dave Tucker, at least until he went just outside of town to play Junior C for the Hespeler Shamrocks in the fall of 1963.

Hespeler had a Juvenile team that had won the Ontario championship the previous year. Now Dave Tucker was coming to town to help take them over the top in the Junior C ranks. He became the team's captain: "He was a goal scorer. He could put the puck in the net," says one of the team's goalies, Bob Hodges, who went on to become a longtime NHL linesman.

Life with the Shamrocks at the old Hespeler Memorial Arena wasn't without its lessons, even for the team's new star. The Shamrocks were coached by a man named Stan Stoddard. He'd been around; he could have had a shot at pro, according to Hodges. One night after a lacklustre showing Stoddard laid down the law. From that point on he wanted all his players in the dressing room an hour before game time and dressed a half hour before puck drop.

"I'll never forget this," says Hodges. "We were playing Elmira and Tucker comes wandering into the dressing room about twenty minutes before the game to get dressed. Stan comes into the room about five minutes before the game was about to start. He looked around the room and he looked at Tucker and said, 'Take your stuff off.' Tucker looked at him and said, 'What?' The coach said, 'You're no better than anyone else in this room. I told you to be in this dressing room at such-and-such a time. Take your stuff off. You're not playing.'"

Bob—like everyone else—was floored. "We thought, 'Dave Tucker *is* the best player.' We went out on the ice and beat Elmira that day. Dave did not come back for two weeks. I guess he eventually swallowed his pride and after that he was even better. I think that's part of the reason we won that year. Stan taught us to play as a team. Not as individuals."

Tucker scored two goals in the championship-winning game, but his time in Hespeler was over. The next season he took it up a notch. He headed down to St. Thomas, Ontario, to play for the Barons of the Western Ontario Junior B Hockey League. The old WOJBL really packed the fans in. Thousands of fans would come out to watch the Barons and other teams in the loop like the London Nationals, Sarnia Legionnaires, and Chatham Junior Maroons. Dave tore it up in St. Thomas: "I think he had 130-some points. It may have been more. He got over seventy goals," marvels John Beechey, a player who came up just a couple of years behind Dave in the old Galt system.

Tucker did lead the league in scoring that year. He had a goal and an assist in St. Thomas's 3–0 game seven, first-round series win in front of 3,300 fans in Sarnia. That set up a match with the London Nationals in the league final. With more than 5,000 fans looking on in London, Tucker scored a goal in game three but it was not enough, and the Nats won. Then on Sunday, March 14, in front of 3,200 fans in St. Thomas, the Nationals finished the series. They beat the Barons 7–5. Tucker had one goal. And that was pretty much it. He had a chance to become a professional. He just didn't do it.

"A lot of guys from the Western Junior B League were getting offers from the NHL," says Beechey. And Dave was one of them. "I think he went to St. Catherines. They were the Chicago farm team at that time. I don't think he was ever that motivated as I recall. I lost track of him. I know he went to Waterloo Lutheran, which became Wilfrid Laurier University."

Tucker chose an education over hockey. He was just a kid, but it was a life-altering decision. "He did tell me about why he didn't go pro," says his son, Kevin. "I think it had a lot to do with family. Dad didn't come from a lot of money. Dad had three brothers and a sister, so he opted to go to school. He was the only one in his family who decided to go to school. He told me that he just wanted to get ahead. He was the only Tucker to actually go to university."

It is easy to see why Dave Tucker didn't pursue a pro career. It's not like he was going to strike it rich coming out of Junior B. John Beechey signed a pro deal; he had offers to attend five of the then six NHL training camps at the time. The only team he didn't get an offer from was the New York Rangers. But he attended their camp in Kitchener as a walk-on. The Rangers liked what they saw and signed him to a C-form, which meant the Rangers owned his NHL rights. "I got a hundred bucks and I eventually got invites to a few more of their training camps. They kept me on the C-form for about eight years. So, I got a hundred bucks a year from New York."

Eight hundred bucks for eight years is not breaking the bank. Beechey thinks Tucker could have gotten a pro contract, easily: "Oh, absolutely, he was good enough. I don't know what it was. It was just his nature. I don't think he wanted that competitive hockey. Now that's only my opinion. He could easily have made our team. No question about it."

Beechey's team became the Galt Hornets. They were the top Senior team in the area. Although the New York Rangers owned his NHL rights, Beechey kept playing locally. The Hornets were a Canadian Senior hockey juggernaut. They won the Allan Cup in 1969 and 1971. The guys on the team would occasionally ask Tucker to play for them. It did not happen. "We would ask him every once in a while, but he was in teacher's college, and he wanted to stay there."

Why did they want Dave on the ice? It's simple: he was a damn fine hockey player. "I've used this comparison before, when I've talked about Dave over the years. He was Gretzky before Gretzky," says Beechey. "But you got to have that motivation."

Beechey, now an accountant for the OHL's Guelph Storm,

did eventually end up playing with Dave, on an old-timers team. Tucker still had it: "He was about six foot one. A straight-up skater, a Gordie Howe type of skater: effortless. He had great, great hands and great command of the rink. He was like a Gretzky on the rink. He knew where everybody was, and where they were going next. Uncanny. He could move the puck freely. And when he had the opportunity, he could shoot!"

Kevin got to see his father's skills as well. He'd hit the ice with Dave and Dave's old buddies. The young kid was still amazed by his old man. "He was quite good. He had very good hands even though he was a little older than some of the guys. The guys would pull me aside and say, 'Your dad is something special. If you can be half as good as him, you're doing well.' I heard it all the time."

Dave Tucker had a patented move that he would pull off. It was called the Tucker Taint: "You know when a guy comes in on his off-wing, like [Jaromir] Jagr used to do. You're coming on your off-wing, and you fake a shot to get the goalie out of the net. Then you fake like you're going behind the net on your backhand and then you pull the puck back and tuck it behind the goalie's pad. Dad would do that a thousand times a game. It was ridiculous. No one could catch it. It was Dad's move. It was the Tucker Taint move. That's what the guys called it."

Kevin is chuckling as he tells of his father's magical moves. He grew up playing in his shadow but that was more than okay with him. Dave Tucker became a high school principal in Kitchener. He followed his son to rinks throughout Ontario, and even showed up in Saginaw, witnessing the insanity of lower-level professional hockey. It was the hockey he regretted not playing, but now his son was. You name it, he saw it: brawls, suspensions,

Zamboni drivers in goal. "He came to a couple of games, and he asked me, 'Just exactly what is this?' Then he said, 'Why don't you try to go to Europe? I should've gone. I had a chance, but anyways . . .' I think Dad was just happy that I tried it and I wouldn't regret anything."

Kevin Tucker played professional hockey for two seasons. He has been in the oil and gas industry in Calgary for years. For Dave Tucker, hockey was always around, even if it wasn't the pros. "Hockey was all we talked about. That was our bond. His passion for the game ran pretty deep. Then as a person I guess he would've been remembered as a teacher, as a disciplinarian. I feel like sometimes he was misunderstood because he was an authoritarian type as a teacher. I always felt he had a big heart. He was always good with me."

David Tucker passed away on August 9, 2018. He was seventy-three years old. A lot of kids who grew up in the Kitchener area likely knew him as Mr. Tucker. He was a teacher, counselor, principal, and dean at St. Jerome's, St. David's, and St. Benedict's high schools. "His hockey skills were great but his skills in mentorship must've been as good because he was able to do what he did," says John Beechey.

Hockey always remained a part of Dave Tucker's life, even though he didn't go pro. He kept playing all the way into his later years and he was a hockey dad to his son, Kevin, who was "Dave Tucker's kid" when he played minor hockey. "I wore it proudly. Being his kid—I thought it was great. I'd hear so much about my dad. Even the wives of my dad's friends would say, 'I remember watching your father play. Your father was just unbelievable.' I heard it all the time. So I wore it with pride. I liked it."

There are still the odd memories of Dave Tucker the hockey

player around Cambridge. His Hespeler Junior C team, which won the Ontario championship in 1964, is in the Cambridge Sports Hall of Fame. In a team picture, Dave is right in the middle. His hair is slicked back. But for young Dave Tucker in that photo, it's a life in teaching, not a life in hockey, that's not too far down the road. Professionally, at least. But he never lost his love of the game, a love and a passion he passed on to his son. On the phone, Kevin tells me this, twice: "Every time I'm out playing hockey I think of my dad."

Dave Tucker in action from his days with Waterloo.

CHAPTER 8

Paul Polillo

Brantford, Ontario

There isn't a hockey fan on the planet who hasn't heard of Brantford, Ontario. The reason: Wayne Gretzky. About a half hour's drive from Hamilton, Brantford is the little city that produced the greatest hockey player the world has ever seen. But there's more to Brantford's hockey story than just Wayne. The city has produced more than a few NHLers, including Wayne's youngest brother, Brent, Adam Henrique, Doug Jarvis, Keith Jones, Chris Gratton, and many others. If you dig a little deeper and ask around, another name will pop up, too. "Paul is not quite a ghost; he's more of a legend," says former OHL head coach Troy Smith. "He's a guy that the old guys at Tim Hortons still talk about. As in, 'Oh, you should've seen this guy, Paul Polillo.' Paul is folklore. That's the way I would put it."

Troy Smith comes from a hockey family. His father, Dave, spent countless hours scouting and watching the game in rinks across southern Ontario. He has seen all kinds of players: fast ones, tough ones, big ones, and small ones. And yes, he has seen Paul Polillo. "I hate to make this comparison," Dave begins, "but Paul was kind of Gretzky-like. He was very special. They played a very similar style. Paul was one of those players who never seemed to be able to be contained by anybody. People would say he never got hit. I'd tell these folks, 'It's not like players didn't try to hit him, they did.' But it's like trying to hit a rope or something. Paul was that elusive. He was a very good skater. He had vision, a hockey sense, that you wouldn't believe. He could find anybody, anywhere, and set them up. And he also could score goals. He scored some beautiful goals. He didn't like taking penalty shots, but he always seemed to score on them. A few times on a penalty shot I saw him start skating from centre and wind up for a slapshot and pick the top corner. It was that easy for Paul," Dave says with a laugh.

"People are going to criticize me for comparing him to Wayne Gretzky," Dave continues. "And I get it. I'm just saying they were very much alike in the style they played. I'm not saying he was as good or better or anything like that. To be clear, I'm not saying that, but they played a very similar style. Paul would go down that left wing and create space and go almost to the top of the circle and then make that great pass just like Wayne would do. And Paul would come down the right wing and make what I called the 'Gretzky move.' He would get to the top of the circle and then cut to the slot and score a goal. He would do that. I've never really asked Paul if he ever patterned his game after Wayne."

"Absolutely. Everything I did in hockey was influenced by Wayne Gretzky," says Paul Polillo, who grew up, like millions of other young hockey players, idolizing Gretzky. But instead of idolizing Wayne from thousands of miles away, Paul was right in the middle of it all. In fact, many times he was sitting in the same house that Wayne once sat in. Paul, six years younger than Wayne, grew up playing minor hockey with Wayne's younger brother Keith. "I wanted to do everything like Wayne. I had a short Titan stick, long tongues on my skates, everything. There are great hockey players today, but Wayne completely changed the whole way hockey was played. I had one of those big satellite dishes at home that my parents bought so we used to watch all the games. It was the wow factor every time you watched."

Paul was what hockey types like to call a late bloomer. While his minor hockey teammate Keith went off to the OHL at just sixteen years of age, Paul hung around Brantford. Instead of playing in the bright hockey spotlight of the Ontario Hockey League, Paul spent his Junior career in his hometown of Brantford. His point totals were not spectacular. He had 25 points in his first year of Junior hockey with the Junior B Brantford Alexander B's. The next year, Paul put up 48 points in 27 games with Brantford and another 20 in 12 games with the Niagara Falls Canucks.

The following year, though, he really took off. He led the Junior B Brantford Classics with 103 points in 38 games. The hockey world took notice, or at least Western Michigan University did. Still sliding under the radar and still blooming, Paul finally left his hometown. He was going five hours away to play for the Western Michigan University Broncos. As a freshman he put up an impressive 66 points, and as a sophomore he led the team with 85 points in 42 games. The twenty-one-year-old had finally bloomed. The Pittsburgh Penguins took him with the fourth pick of the 1988 NHL Supplemental Draft.

The Supplemental Draft should have been called the "Late Bloomers Draft." It lasted for almost a decade, from 1986 to 1994. It was created to cut down on bidding wars for undrafted college players. In other words, late bloomers or players that teams had missed out on the first time around. A new NHL collective bargaining agreement put an end to the Supplemental Draft by the mid-1990s, but in the late 1980s, Paul Polillo finally got a little respect from the NHL brains when he became property of the Pittsburgh Penguins. He spent two more years with the Broncos and decided to go pro after his fourth season in Kalamazoo, Michigan. Making the Penguins roster was the plan, but things changed. A player needs a lot of things to go right for him to make it to the NHL. One of them is for others to believe in him. General Manager Tony Esposito in Pittsburgh did when they took Polillo in the 1988 Supplemental Draft, but by the time Paul decided to go pro in 1990, the Espositos were out in Pittsburgh. Craig Patrick was now the Pens' general manager. "I was thinking that Pittsburgh was going to sign me, and I was going to do what I had to do to go there," says Paul. "I talked with Patrick, and he said, 'We haven't had much time to do scouting. We are just going to let you come to camp and see what happens.'"

In other words, the Penguins were not going to offer the then twenty-three-year-old Polillo a guaranteed contract. There was no money on the table. Polillo already had a backup plan in place. His father, Guy, had immigrated to Canada many years before. Guy came to Canada with nothing. His first job in Canada was shining shoes. Now he ran a successful business in Brantford called Classic Home Improvements. Paul's plan, if the Pens weren't going to offer him a contract up front, was to do the opposite of what his dad did. He was going to go from Canada to Italy and play professionally in his father's homeland. "I actually had a deal to go to Europe for three years and I said to Patrick, 'If you at least match my deal in Europe then I will come to Pittsburgh. If I have to go to Muskegon [the minors] or whatever, I'll do it. But the Penguins said, 'No, we want you to just try out.'"

Paul told the Pens that he was choosing Europe over a camp invite from Pittsburgh. "I actually have a copy of the letter I sent them. I said, 'I hope you guys win the Cup this year.' To be honest, I was feeling a little bit snotty about it. But they actually did win the Cup," he laughs.

He had a three-year deal with Latemar in Italy. Paul did what was expected of him—he put up ridiculous numbers: 103 points in 34 games. Life in Italy was good; so good, in fact, that when the Penguins offered him another chance to go back, he said, no thanks. "I told the Penguins, 'I still have this deal in Europe.' My thought at the time was if I go to Pittsburgh, I have no bargaining power whatsoever. They can just do whatever they want with me. I thought if they were interested in me, they could at least offer me something on paper. They didn't."

With no written offer from the Pens, Paul stayed in Italy for a second season. He led the team in scoring again, with a mere (by his standards) 57 points in 28 games. The Pens won another Cup. When the fall of 1992 rolled around, Paul Polillo's plan was to head back to Italy. There was just one problem. His team folded. The twenty-four-year-old had no place to play. What was a scoring machine from Brantford to do? There was only one answer— go home.

Brantford had always had hockey teams, mostly Junior and Senior ones, such as the Foresters and the Major Junior Alexanders. But by the mid-1990s, there was professional hockey in town. The Brantford Smoke joined the Colonial Hockey League in the fall of 1991. A group of local businessmen decided to put together the team. Of course, they had to think of a name for the team. Brantford was joining a league with teams named the Falcons, the Thunderhawks, and the Bulldogs. Brantford went with Smoke: "There was a guy named Vic Porter who was a local intermediate and Senior player at one time," begins Dave Smith, who served as the Smoke's general manager and director of player operations for a season. "He knew my dad from the car business. My dad told me a bunch of guys were sitting around one day trying to figure out what to call the team. Vic smoked cigars, and he took a big draw from a big Cuban cigar and blew the smoke out and said, 'I think we have it: the Brantford Smoke.' And that's how the team got named. Great name."

The Smoke began their second season in the seven-team Colonial Hockey League with a hometown boy at centre. Paul Polillo was going to try his luck at home. And so began the legend. His point totals in the Colonial League don't just jump off the page at you, they hit you like a slapshot off your chin. Year one: 112 points and a league championship. Year two: 141. Year three: 146. Year four: 186. Year five: 173. Year six: 165. Troy Smith was a young defenceman playing in the OHL when he first set eyes on Polillo and at the time his father was the GM of the Smoke. "My dad started talking about this guy and I went out and watched this Polillo guy play. He was friggin' unbelievable. He had no business being in the Colonial Hockey League. I didn't really understand at that time why he would stay there, considering all the points he was getting."

Polillo was doing in the Colonial Hockey League what his idol Wayne Gretzky did in the NHL for all those years. He was not only winning the scoring championship, but he was also destroying the competition. In his third year in the league, he won the scoring title by 53 points. "There was an energy about the guy when he was on the ice," says David. "Everybody kind of perked up and watched to see what he was going to do." Sound familiar?

As Troy said, from the outside, by just looking at the stats alone, Paul had no business playing in the Colonial League. When you put up numbers like Polillo did, you move up to a higher league. At least that's how the hockey world works most of the time. The brass at the Smoke would get calls from teams in the AHL or calls from teams in the IHL looking for Paul to move up. One day in the 1994–95 season, Paul decided to give it a go. "I actually did go to the IHL for one game. I think it really soured me on it. I got a phone call from the coach of the Denver Grizzlies."

The team gave Polillo their plan. The Grizzlies were playing that night in Milwaukee. The team needed Paul to drive from Brantford to Toronto and hop on a flight to Milwaukee. That's what he did. Kevin Cheveldayoff, who is now the general manager of the Winnipeg Jets, picked Paul up at the Milwaukee airport. The high-scoring forward suited up and was ready to go. "I go all that way . . . for three shifts. And then I come home, and I thought, 'I'm never, ever going to go through this again.' I couldn't believe it—all that fuss for three shifts. At that time the guys weren't as welcoming as they are now. I went to go sit on the bus and someone said, 'Hey, man, this seat is taken.' I'm not nineteen years old anymore. I'm twenty-five at the time and it just soured me. I remember thinking, 'I'm having so much fun playing in Brantford. I make decent money. My wife can work and everything like that. I've got kids. Why do I need this shit?'"

That was it for the IHL. Married to his high school sweetheart and raising a family, Polillo decided to stay at home. Like he said, the money was good. "I was making just as much as guys were in the American League." He could (and did) live in his own house. He worked for his dad's company, Classic Home Improvements, in the off-season, and was still the "Gretzky of the Colonial League" in the winters. (In fact, he even wore the old JOFA helmet.) And just like number 99, he had some muscle riding shotgun on his wing.

"We had a pretty good coach—Larry Trader—who had spent some time in the NHL," remembers David Smith. "Larry seemed to find the guys who could play with Paul. There was always a physical guy with him, but not just a physical guy. This was a player who could also score if Paul could set him up. A couple of the guys come to mind, like Herb Raglan. He was a former NHLer who we brought in."

Raglan was tough. He was a guy who had been around the NHL block. How tough? "He was on Don Cherry's *Rock'em Sock'em 8* or something like that," Dave says with a chuckle. Playing alongside Polillo, Raglan scored 46 goals and 38 assists for 84 points in the 1995–96 season. He also had a staggering 267 minutes in the penalty box. Just as number 99 had Semenko or McSorley, Polillo had Raglan. That kind of toughness, having that cop on your wing, can make a point producer feel pretty safe about going about his job. "Absolutely," says Polillo. "Herb is tough as nails. Back in those days you could use your stick a little more than you can now. Nobody wanted to mess with him."

Except the Flint Generals mascot. Dave Smith is laughing as he tells me this story: "It was a Friday night in Flint. Flint was a nasty place to play. The fans are on top of you. It was a ruckus, and they hated the opposition. The referee, Dave Peel, let everything go. It was horrible. We had about eight or nine penalties in the first period. Flint had a mascot called the General. It was huge. It must've been, I don't know, twelve feet high. It was one of those blowup costumes that you blow up with the compressor."

The General was huge, and the General was mouthy. Most mascots do not say a word. But that night the General decided to sound off. With his underlings in tow, holding his twelve-foot body high above the Smoke, he sounded off and let the guys from Brantford know just what he and Flint thought of them after the first period came to an end. "As our players are skating off the ice," Dave continues, "the mascot came up to us bobbling along. He was after our players. I don't know what he said, I was way up high watching. I could see our players were a little annoyed by the whole situation."

Raglan had had enough, and as Paul reminds us, in the mid-1990s you could get away with a little more with your stick. Herb speared the General. That is not a typo. "Herb spears this mascot," continues Dave, who all these years later still doesn't seem overly sympathetic toward the General. "I said, 'Okay, that's fine.' Halfway through the intermission I noticed the mascot is starting to keel over and they've got ten or twelve people trying to hold the thing up. The spear had caused a leak in the costume—they had to get a local tire company to come and patch him up and blow it back up."

While all this was going on, Paul Polillo kept scoring. Wherever he went, he was the show. He was the superstar the fans came to see. "Paul was as well-known in the other markets as he was here in Brantford," says Dave. "You go on the road and all the people wanted to talk about was Paul Polillo, what makes him so good, what about this, what about that. He was that kind of player."

Travel in the Colonial Hockey League was not fun or easy. "You've got the Quad Cities [in Illinois and Iowa]; Madison, Wisconsin; Utica, New York. Some of those bus trips were horrendous."

The longest trip was the eighteen-hour journey on the "Iron Lung" to Thunder Bay. Eighteen hours there, eighteen hours back. And once you got to Thunder Bay, it was three games in four nights. On the phone, Dave tells me there was no team that tried to take the "Colonial Gretzky" off his game more than the Thunder Bay Senators. They were a heavily armed bunch, with the likes of Bruce Ramsay, who spent six-plus seasons in the Colonial League, once racking up 463 PIM in a single season. There was another legendary minor-league toughie for the Thunder Bay Sens who always did his best to try to slow down Polillo. "The guys in Thunder Bay, for sure, they were the ones that tried the hardest not to hurt Paul or anything, but to take him out of his game and they couldn't do it. And they had some tough guys. My God, Mel Angelstad was on that team. And there were a few others. As much as they tried to take Paul out of the game, they couldn't do it."

Despite his brief, sour tenure with the Grizzlies in the IHL, teams in the "I" kept calling. Paul kept saying no. The Chicago Wolves called and offered Paul a contract. It was no use. He was staying at home. It may sound strange to anyone not named Paul Polillo, but climbing the hockey ladder, grinding it out despite what others might think, just wasn't for him. He was content to play at home, to be at home, year after year after year. "I had a young family and I had been running around with hockey all my life, doing a lot of things. I love to play hockey. That is something you will never get rid of. But I had everything that I wanted right here in Brantford. I played and we had great times. It was a lot of fun."

Another Gretzky comparison: try to think of the best Gretzky play . . . is that even possible? Dave Smith comes to the same conclusion about Paul. "One play? No, I don't think there is one play because I'll tell you, just when you think you've seen him make the greatest Polillo play, he would make one that was better. It was just incredible. How did he see that guy? How did he get the puck through? Just when you were thinking, 'He's all alone, surrounded by the opposing players, no way is he going to score. No way.' But, somehow, he did. Five-hole. On the ice it didn't matter what you did, he knew what to do."

Could he have made it? The scouts thought so. At least that's what they told the team's general manager: "I had several NHL scouts that I talked to, and I did a little scouting myself for Major Junior and some of the minor pros and whatnot, they would talk to me about Paul, and they would say, 'You know what? He could play in the NHL.' There was hardly a scout that didn't say that. It was just amazing."

As if that's not enough, Smith tells me Polillo even had endorsements from a Hall of Famer and a member of the legendary 1972 Team Canada. "Harry Howell and Pat Stapleton were good friends of mine, and they both said, 'This guy can play in the NHL. He's that good.' Anyway, I know it's just an opinion but those are two guys who knew what real hockey was."

What does Paul think? I decided to ask him. "I get that question all the time. A lot of people don't realize what it takes to play in the NHL. They all say, 'Oh, you should've played in the NHL,' and all that. But it's one thing saying it and there's another thing doing it. I'll tell you this. If the game was played the way it is today, then I could probably play in the NHL. But it was a different kind of game then. To be a guy to play like me, you had to have Wayne Gretzky numbers. And to do that in the Colonial Hockey League and to do that in the NHL are two different things. They [the NHL] wanted big strong guys. And you had to have the right situation and people around it to be a guy like Wayne Gretzky. They don't give a shit about me. I haven't done anything that big. But I'm a firm believer that in today's game I could've played. I'm sure I could probably give it a go because there are a lot of smaller guys in the game. The game has changed to where it is all skill."

It was not all skill in Paul's day. He was a 5'11", 178-pound centre who skated with a JOFA helmet, Perfecta blades, and an eye for the game in the Colonial. Another guy from Brantford was a 6', 185-pound centre who skated with a JOFA helmet, Perfecta blades, and an eye for the game in the NHL. They were both the Gretzkys of their league, except the latter did it in the best league in the world, and the former did it in his hometown. If you're wondering, Paul did get to meet Wayne, at least in passing, a couple of times. There's a legendary story from the 1987 Canada Cup: A few of the Soviet players went to the Gretzky house in Brantford for a barbecue and a few pops during the tournament. Polillo found himself at the Gretzky home as well. "Keith said to me, 'Do you want to go to the game?' It was an exhibition game, at Copps Coliseum [in Hamilton] against the Russians. So, Keith picks me up at my parents' house. There was a girl in the front seat. Keith said, 'Oh, this is my brother's girlfriend, Janet.' I didn't know who she was. We went to the game, and she came home with Wayne, and we went back to the Gretzky house and all the Russian guys were there. I remember Dave Poulin [from Team Canada] was there. A bunch of other Canada guys. I met Wayne a few times like that, just in passing, but I tell you what, he's one of those guys that I really would like to meet."

No matter how old you are, your hockey idols are still your idols. That goes for Polillo, too. He ended up playing Senior hockey around the Brantford area until he was well into his thirties. He now runs Classic Home Improvements. He still dreams of maybe cracking a pop or two with the guy he modeled his game after. "I still have dreams about meeting Wayne . . . and I'm fifty-five years old. It's weird, I sometimes think that we're friends," Paul says laughing. "It's crazy, but I'm still a huge fan of his."

Two Brantford boys. "At the height of the Smoke's popularity," says Dave Smith, "Paul was right up there with Wayne. He

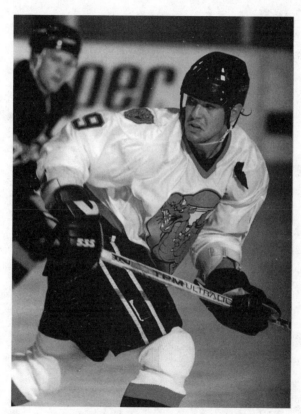

Paul Polillo, doing his best to look the
part of his idol, Wayne Gretzky, as a
member of the Brantford Smoke.

was that good. I lived in Hamilton at the time, and I played on an old-timers team. I would have guys ask me about him, 'This Polillo guy, is he really that good?' I said, 'Watch the games. You'll see.' And then they would come out to a game and watch him and say, 'Holy mackerel! This guy is amazing.' He was well-known in Brantford. There's no question about it among hockey people. To this day in Brantford, if you mention Paul's name, they all light up. Wayne is Wayne, no question. But Polillo is an amazing second place. One of the best, ever, from Brantford."

CHAPTER 9

George Pelawa

Bemidji, Minnesota

If you've ever been to an NHL game you've heard the song. If you've ever closed your eyes and fantasized, just for a second, about playing even a single shift in the NHL—or tied up your skates on a cold winter day and taken a few awkward steps through crunching snow to a perfectly clean sheet of frozen ice— you understand the weight of those lyrics.

Tom Cochrane's "Big League" is a song about chasing the hockey dream. A dream that has a tragic ending.

"We always believed at home that the song was about George. But no one ever really found out," says Steve Peters, a hockey lifer who grew up in the small town of Bemidji, Minnesota.

He is talking about George Pelawa. George died in a car accident just a couple of months after the Calgary Flames took the hulking 6'3", 240-pound forward with the sixteenth pick in the 1986 NHL Draft. He was just weeks away from starting his first season of his NCAA career at the University of North Dakota.

"George was this mammoth individual from Bemidji, the home of Paul Bunyan," remembers Al Coates, who was a member of the Flames front office when they drafted Pelawa. "If Paul

Bunyan had shown up at training camp instead of George, I'm not sure we would've known the difference. He was really something. He was as raw as they come."

Over the years George's story, just like Paul Bunyan's, has become the stuff of legend. A large statue of Paul Bunyan, the towering lumberjack, and his constant companion Babe the Blue Ox sits in Bemidji right on the shores of Lake Bemidji. George was a kid who skated on those lakes, who would one day grow into a gigantic forward for the Bemidji High School Lumberjacks hockey team.

"I think Bemidji is probably a lot like small-town Canada," says Peters about his hometown. "It's so far from the Minneapolis–St. Paul area that you don't think of the big city. When the weather is cold, you get on a lake and you play hockey. It's just a small community where everybody knows everybody that's involved in sports. Life was slow and easy back in the seventies and eighties, way before cell phones and all that. It was a great place to grow up because it wasn't the hustle and bustle of the big city. It was a really small-town feel. I've got a lot of Canadian relatives and that's what it reminded me of. If you took a small-town Canadian kid, you could go to Bemidji, and you'd fit right in."

For kids like Steve and George, who grew up in Bemidji back then, sports were the thing to do. It was baseball in the summer, football in the fall, and hockey in the winter. And when you got to your teenaged years, the best hockey to play was Minnesota high school hockey: "Everybody wanted to play for the high school team in a small town like Bemidji," says Peters. "It was similar to playing in Juniors in Canada. It was a big deal to play for the high school team. You play in front of 1,500 fans and you're playing at the Bemidji State College Arena. It was big-time to play for your local high school. You saw high school hockey as a path. If you could be really good in Minnesota high school hockey you might get the opportunity to move on and play college hockey. People in Bemidji just weren't aware of Canadian Junior hockey. Your goal as a kid was to play for your high school team in front of your friends."

When George Pelawa started his high school career, he was far away from the hype machine of today's young prospects. In fact, he was pretty far away from first-line duty with the Bemidji Lumberjacks, a public school team made up of Pelawa, Peters, and their buddies from around town. "To be honest, George wasn't very good," says Peters, a goalie on the team. "It's not one of those stories where the five-year-old kid goes up and down the ice and scores every goal. That wasn't George. You knew when he was on the ice because he was a big kid, but he didn't skate very well, and he didn't have the skills then. Even when he was fifteen, his sophomore year in high school, you started to think, 'Okay, maybe.' But he still wasn't one of the better kids on the team, and this was a town of ten thousand people. The NHL? You're out of your mind. He's a third-line player on a small-town high school team. There's no way that this kid is going to play past high school."

George didn't score a single goal as a sophomore. By the time the next season rolled around he'd gone through a growth spurt, but it wasn't ordinary. There was no awkwardness. He didn't grow six inches into a skinny high school beanpole who'd forgotten how to use his hands and feet. His whole body grew. Before you knew it, the kid who was on the third line as a sophomore was a giant: a real-life Paul Bunyan. There was no one bigger on the ice for Bemidji High School in winter 1984–85.

"By the time he got to be a junior in high school he was a beast," says Peters, who watched all this magic from his crease. "It was like a light switch. Now this is where legend starts to come in. I remember him as 6'3", 240 pounds. Our team mascot was the Lumberjack, and it was fitting because he was Paul Bunyan. George was bigger than life. When you walked into a hockey arena with George, people noticed."

When you're that size, with speed to match, domination will soon follow. Both scoring and physical domination: "If you can skate and you're six-three, 240, and you're playing against fifteen-year-olds that are probably 125 pounds, it was dangerous," Peters tells me. "George wasn't out to hurt you. He just hit really, really hard. It was the maturation from a kid who was fourteen or fifteen, not sure if he'd make his high school team, to a nationally recognized player."

He led the Lumberjacks in scoring with 26 goals in his junior year: "I have never seen anybody with a physical presence in the state tournament like Pelawa," Minnesota North Stars general manager Lou Nanne told the Minneapolis *Star Tribune* after Bemidji High was eliminated in the 1985 state tourney. "That is strength."

It was strength and it was raw skill. And that was it for George's hockey until next season. He didn't spend his summer shooting pucks in the driveway. He did other things, like any other kid. And in the winter, when his team wasn't practicing, he wasn't on the outdoor rinks in town doing drills. He'd be out playing friendly hockey with his buddies. There was no intense training. George was playing, just for fun, but all of this was taking him somewhere. "George experienced life. He was just naturally good at hockey. You wonder where he could've gone if he would've applied himself a little bit more, but then he wouldn't have been who he was," says Peters.

As a high school senior, George dominated in front of 1,500 fans. He was the local hero. One game that stands out in Peters's mind was against their rivals from Hibbing High School: "We were playing at home. There was a full crowd. It was the end of the season. We are both probably going to go to the state tournament to compete for the state championship. And George just took the game over. It was almost like he was swatting flies around their net. I don't recall exactly how many goals he got. I know he scored in that game. But you just remember him being in the slot and there was no one around him because you couldn't be around him. He would just push you out of the way. His command of the puck and his ability to get space was not normal for Minnesota high school. It was not normal for any high school player to have that kind of domination. And he could skate. I remember him getting a big goal and we said to each other on the bench, 'That's why we have George. That's why we're so good. That's why we're winning.' George had that crowd on their feet with his arms over his head. We ended up beating one of the best teams in the state that year in one of the final home games of our high school career. That was the pinnacle of what George brought to the hockey team."

The Lumberjacks did indeed meet Hibbing again in the state tournament, but that time the Bluejackets came out on top. They beat the Lumberjacks 4–3 in the state quarterfinals in front of an incredible 17,759 fans. Remember that this is a high school hockey game. The Minnesota North Stars of the NHL averaged 13,215 that same year, 1985–86, playing in the same building. Pelawa had a goal and an assist in the loss. The *Star Tribune* described his goal this way: "Pelawa scored at 6:14, crashing to the net with enough force to take a defender, Hibbing goalie Jim Monacelli and the puck into the cage."

A fitting end to his high school career. George was named Mr. Hockey for the state of Minnesota. He set Bemidji High School records with 29 goals and 25 assists, totaling 54 points! The previous record holder was Gary Sargent, who played more than 400 games in the NHL. Surely that's where George was headed.

George wasn't done with his season; he had a showcase tournament to play in. "There's a story and I don't know how you could ever verify it," says Peters. "In our senior year there was a high school showcase and he played for Team Minnesota, and he put a guy through the glass and broke his collarbone and his arm by pushing him through the glass. I wasn't there. I don't know if it's true."

That's the type of story legends are made of. Like all good folklore tales, it may be true, but we do know this: a showcase tournament is where the Calgary Flames first laid eyes on George. The tournament was in Texas. Jack Ferreira, the future GM of the Anaheim Ducks, was the Flames' chief American scout. Perhaps he had an early eye on George. There was no better organization in hockey in the 1980s at identifying young American players than the Flames.

Al MacNeil was at the tournament scouting for the Flames: "When Al went down to Houston, I don't think he went specifically to look at George, just to look at the tournament," says Al Coates, the Flames' assistant GM at the time. "But he came back and talked to Cliff [Fletcher, the Flames' GM] and me about this monstrous seventeen- or eighteen-year-old kid—six foot three or four, two hundred and some pounds already. The interesting thing was the size of George's feet. For a big man he wore eight-and-a-half-size skates. Which was crazy for a man that size."

Just who was this kid? Soon enough the Flames found out that

Pelawa had committed to play hockey at the University of North Dakota. That story had a legendary twist to it, too. The Flames got word through the grapevine that he had made a pretty good impression on the North Dakota staff when he stumbled upon a weight room during a UND recruiting trip. George looked at the weights and asked the recruiters what they were. He was told the weights were for football players. "So, George says, 'I want to try it.' Over he goes and there's 235, 240, and 255 pounds on the bench press and he just rips off about a dozen, and they say, 'Oh my God,'" Coates tells me.

The Flames were a stacked team in 1986. They had just lost in the Stanley Cup Finals to the Montreal Canadiens. They had the sixteenth pick in the draft. With a pick that deep in the first round, Coates says the Flames were never shy to "take a flyer on somebody." They'd go for the big score. George Pelawa was raw, he came out of nowhere, but he would be so tough to pass up with the sixteenth pick for a team that was already loaded with top-notch talent. "It was maybe a bit of a reach, but where teams drafted then and still today, in that particular part of the draft, you are reaching for something that is hopefully going to be special."

Pelawa was drafted in the Montreal Forum in the first round of the NHL Draft on June 21, 1986. Pelawa was chosen ahead of players like Adam Graves, Teppo Numminen, and Lyle Odelein. A little over two years before, he had just finished his sophomore season of high school hockey in Bemidji, with a grand total of zero goals. That must have been a hell of a feeling. The Flames put on a little shindig for their draft picks and their families on the top floor of the Sheraton after the draft. "I think we had half of the top floor of the hotel," says Coates. George came up to the room. Soon enough he was offered a beer. "He grabbed a beer and that thing was gone in a second or two." George grabbed another one. It was gone in a flash as well. The boys told George that was probably enough for now.

A minute or two later Coates took a second to gaze out a window at the city of Montreal. Then he looked down at the street. "I see this guy bolting across the street. He tries to jump over a fence. He catches the tip of his toe on the top of the fence rail. Down he goes. Headfirst into the parking lot on the other side. And it was George."

The next stop for George was the University of North Dakota. He wasn't the only Bemidji kid going to UND. Steve Peters was also recruited for the team, along with another one of their Lumberjacks teammates, Darryn Fossand. All three made their way to UND in August to get used to college life. They had one last free weekend before the team got down to business. George figured it would be a perfect time to head home. "George stopped in my dorm room and he told me, 'Hey, I'm going home for a high school party.' And I said, 'Let's stay here for a college party.' I didn't go home, and George went. He never came back," says Peters.

That Friday, George headed home to Bemidji. He and his brother Joe went out that night. At two in the morning, on Saturday, August 30, George and his brother were in an accident with another car on a county road five miles outside of Bemidji. George was a passenger in the car. A *Star Tribune* report said George was thrown through the windshield of the car and bled to death from a severed artery.

"I'm lucky I didn't go," says Peters. "I wish I could've talked him out of it. I wish we would've said, 'Don't go. Don't go home.' I've had that conversation a lot with myself over the years. I wish we could've done more. We didn't. But you don't know. You don't think this is the last time you're going to see that person. That was hard. That was a hard time."

Al Coates got the news early in the morning. The first thing he did was get in touch with his team's general manager, Cliff Fletcher. "We made arrangements. Badger [head coach Bob Johnson], Cliff, me, we all chartered down for the funeral. I remember Neil Sheehy and Gary Suter and two or three other players went commercial through Minneapolis to be there for the funeral."

The town was in shock. The hockey world was in shock. When death hits kids for the first time, they don't know what to do. Peters headed home to Bemidji right away: "We went to the funeral, which was incredibly hard. And really hard for his family. A bunch of the kids from my grade, the graduating class, we went out in front of the high school late at night. We didn't know what to do or where to focus our attention. We took a bedsheet and we painted on it, 'WE MISS YOU GEORGE.' We went and we hung out on the front of the high school. We just sat there. We just sat there on the grass in front of the high school. It was a cold Minnesota night. We sat there for hours. Cars would drive by and honk their horns and we would wave. We just sat there and told stories about George. George touched everybody out in front of that school. It wasn't just the hockey players that were there. There were different groups of people who were all there just to pay respect to their friend. And that's one of the things that was a testament to George. He was a great football player. He was a great baseball player. But he was more than that. He was just involved with everyone. He was a Bemidji kid. He was ours. He belonged to us. I think that legend—we still see it today. His jersey is retired at the Bemidji High School, the number eight. The legend still grows. He is still talked about today. He's that Paul Bunyan type figure."

George Pelawa's story is the ultimate "What if?" What could he have become? The big raw kid from Bemidji was off to suit up for UND. What would college have been like for him? What about after college? Would he have been a Flame the next season? Or would he have played for the United States at the 1988 Olympics in Calgary instead?

"I don't think George thought about the Olympics," Steve tells me. "I don't think he thought much ahead. I know Calgary came up and I know there was a thought process that he [should] go play pro right away. At that time North Dakota was a team that was going to compete for a national championship. And there was a thought that George had some things to work on before he could make that jump physically to the NHL. He was ready, but that's a pretty big jump. I don't think even in his mind he thought he was ready to jump right to the NHL. But I don't think he thought he was going to be at North Dakota for more than a year. Academically, it probably wasn't his thing, going to school. I think he was going to college to be a hockey player. I don't think he would've made it longer than a year."

So maybe a year at UND, then a year in the minors, and then the NHL. In the 1990s the NHL became a big man's league. Every team was desperate for a power forward in their lineup. The Flames would have been way ahead of the curve with their draft pick from 1986. "You don't know," says Coates. "The great unknown is the saddest thing, the loss of life and the great unknown, of what could've been. In that era, with his size . . ." Here Coates trails off, wistfully, before resuming: "I don't think there's any doubt in my mind that kid would've made it."

One player from George's Bemidji High School team did make it all the way to the NHL, but not as a player. Steve Peters was the Arizona Coyotes' video coach for more than twenty years. He started with the team in 1997. George Pelawa would have been, just like Steve, twenty-nine at the time. "George? He would've had a long career in the NHL, with his size and that ability to skate," says his old high school buddy, who now lives in Arizona and works in hockey broadcasting for ESPN. "It would've been interesting to see how much he could've done and what he would've done with the team in Calgary with the way they played. They would've just embraced the guy with his fun-loving personality. Everybody wanted to be around George and that community would've embraced him. Calgary was a perfect spot for George."

As for "Big League"—was it really about George Pelawa? Tom Cochrane told the *National Post* in 2015 that he got the idea for the song when a custodian told him a story when Cochrane was "up north."

George Pelawa, Mr. Hockey Minnesota, 1986.

"He came up and he said, 'My boy's a big fan of "Boy Inside the Man."'" And I said, 'Oh, is he coming to the show? We're playing it tonight,'" Cochrane said. "And he said, 'No, he passed away, he was an aspiring hockey player.'"

Peters often wondered if "Big League" was indeed about his buddy George. In a way, it is. Cochrane also said this to the *National Post*: "I think what's important is that it is inclusive for everybody. I don't think it's that important, specifically, who it's about."

So, in a way, yeah, Steve, it is about George.

CHAPTER 10

Clifford Duchesne

Thompson and The Pas, Manitoba

Thompson, Manitoba, is known as the Hub of the North. Founded in the 1950s, it is about eight hours north of Winnipeg by car. It was a mining town; now around thirteen thousand people live there. With countless frozen ponds and lakes, there is more than enough ice to skate on for a good portion of the year. It's on these outdoor rinks that Clifford Duchesne Jr. honed his hockey skills. And sadly, ultimately, it was one of those waterways that claimed his life.

"Everything's changed quite a bit since that day. Our lives changed," said Clifford Duchesne Sr., a soft-spoken, retired taxi driver from Thompson, who passed away in February 2023.

It is amazing how the smallest thing can change everything. On Christmas Day 2000, twenty-two-year-old Cliff Duchesne Jr. was out on his snowmobile, heading home after a few hours searching for caribou. "He got up and told me he'd heard there was caribou just north of here. He said, 'I'm going to go and look at them caribou,'" explains Cliff Sr. "I told him, 'Maybe you should go to Paint Lake for a ride instead, with another guy.' 'No,' he said, 'I'm going to look at them caribou.' He took off about eleven am."

Later that day, Royal Canadian Mounted Police spokesman Sergeant Steve Saunders described what had happened on a bridge over the Burntwood River as a "tragic, freak accident." Just before three o'clock, around four hours after young Cliff headed out on his brand-new snowmobile, everything changed for the Duchesne family. Cliff was crossing the bridge on his sled when one of its skis got caught in a rail along the sidewalk portion of the bridge. That sent Cliff flying off the machine, over the bridge, and into the cold, fast waters of the Burntwood River. Just think about how fast a river in northern Manitoba has to be running if it is not frozen over by Christmas Day.

Cliff would have done what he always did. He'd have given it everything he had, trying to hang on against the rushing river. Cliff Sr. was at work at the time, driving his taxi. His brother was a cabdriver, too, making his way to Nelson House (seventy-five kilometres northwest of Thompson) when he came across the chaos at the Miles Hart Bridge. "He seen Cliffy's Ski-Doo and Cliff there [in the water]," says Cliff Sr.

A newspaper account from the December 27, 2000, edition of the *Winnipeg Sun* describes what took place: "A friend of Duchesne's and another witness watched from the span as the 22-year-old grabbed on to a small ice floe and was tugged by the current underneath the bridge."

Cliff Sr. raced to the scene. But no one could save his son that Christmas Day. "We met right at the Catholic church. We pulled in there. My brother, he told me, 'That's Cliffy in the water. He's . . . gone,'" says Cliff Sr., still fighting to find the words more than two decades later.

Divers couldn't even enter the water to search for Cliff's body.

The high speed of the river simply made it too dangerous. A twenty-two-year-old kid, a son, a brother, and a hockey hero, was gone.

Young Cliff Duchesne wasn't an overly big kid. His father didn't play hockey, but once upon a time, when little Cliff was around seven years old, the topic came up. "One day I was having coffee with a fellow I worked with. He said, 'My boy is playing cross-ice hockey. You should bring your boy.' I said, 'I will.' And I did. He never skated before, but then he got on the ice, and he just went. He wouldn't quit," says Cliff Sr.

"He wouldn't quit" is what everyone told me about Cliff Jr. This kid had the kind of insatiable appetite for the game that simply cannot be taught. His father told me, "When he was seven or eight years old, he tried out in the fall for a team. They said he wasn't good enough. So, he played cross-ice hockey."

Cross-ice hockey is a way for kids to start the game. The game is played exactly as it sounds. Instead of using the full 200-foot length of ice, players put the nets on either side of the rink, 85 feet apart, and play across the width of the ice. There are no offsides, no icings. It is a good, fun, but noncompetitive way to get kids used to playing the game.

Cliff Jr. didn't make the big team: he didn't care. He played cross-ice hockey and hit the outdoor rinks, no matter how cold it got. "Cliff was crazy for the outdoor rink. I'd come home from work, and he would be crying if I wouldn't let him go, but it was forty below. He wanted to go out there and skate, so I would take him. I knew the guy at the outdoor arena, and he would say, 'Don't worry, just leave him. I will make sure he comes in and warms up.'"

Cliff wouldn't leave those frigid temperatures to ease the chill, not even for a second. He just kept skating. Soon enough, a kid dropped out of that big team, and Cliff was invited to join for a tournament, five and a half hours away in Lynn Lake, a town not that far from the Saskatchewan-Manitoba border. "Cliff was the star of the tournament. An all-star the first time he ever played," says his father.

Thompson had a new minor hockey star. Cliff kept playing and he kept getting better. "Young Cliffy, when he first started off in hockey, I know there was people that figured he wasn't good enough or he was too small. They bypassed him but that didn't stop Clifford. By the time he was in Peewee, he was winning all the awards and making a name for himself, and not just in our community, but throughout northern Manitoba," says Doug Korman.

Korman lives in Paint Lake now, about twenty minutes outside of Thompson. For twenty-three years he was the head coach of the Norman Northstars, the biggest deal in Thompson hockey. Why the name? Norman stands for northern Manitoba. The team draws players from all over the region, even up into Nunavut. The Norman Northstars are a big deal in Thompson, and by the time Cliff was sixteen, he was old enough to join the team. Cliff was the local boy done good. Most players were from out of town and lived with billets, just for the privilege to play for the Northstars; Cliff stayed right at home. His impact was immediate.

"He had the love of the game," says Korman. "I always preached that in our program, education was number one and hockey was number two. A very close two. Cliff managed to get through the schooling, but hockey was the number one thing in

Cliffy's life. He was the first one at the rink. The hardest worker on the ice. The hardest worker at dry-land training. He had an attraction. His smile, it just lit up a room."

That Clifford Duchesne smile—Korman kept going back to it. It was a smile that would have him—and everyone, really—trying to figure out what the undersized, take-no-prisoners player was up to. "He would make you smile with him just smiling; you wouldn't even have to talk to him. You'd just see his big grin, and you're wondering, is he up to something or is that just his personality? And it was just his personality. I can honestly say coaching him and watching him through minor hockey, he just loved the game. Many of the young kids in town would come out to practice. I'd bring ten-year-olds to come out for a skate occasionally and they all went to young Cliffy. They loved him!"

"The kids who watched him twenty years ago are all grown up now," says Cliff Sr. "They all knew Cliff. Everybody knew him."

One of those kids was Greg Douglas. He is now a hockey dad himself and is stationed with the RCMP in Red Deer, Alberta. Greg used to be one of hundreds of kids in Thompson who jammed into a rink for a Norman Northstars game (*jammed* being the key word). The Norman Northstars weren't your typical AAA Midget team. Thompson didn't have a Junior team to cheer for, and it was not odd to see 2,500 people cheer on the Northstars on a cold Thompson night.

"Cliff was just *the* idol growing up back home," says Douglas. "The Norman Northstars were the only ticket in town. We'd go every Saturday and Sunday. It was always a packed house. When Cliff played, those were the glory days. It was awesome—he was seven or eight years older than me. I was nine or ten, right in that age of having an idol and a hero, and Cliff was a hometown guy."

Ten-year-old Greg saw the same thing everyone else did: "He was just absolutely relentless. It's not like he worked hard every shift. He worked hard every single *play*. He would take the puck out of the corner and battle three or four dudes behind the net and then bury a wraparound. He was relentless."

Cliff scored 15 points in 15 games as a rookie. The next year he had 46 points in 29 games. Then, in his final season with the Northstars, Cliff finished second on the team with 89 points and led the way with 120 penalty minutes. He was a seventeen-year-old local hockey hero. On *Hockey Night in Canada*, you often see kids reaching over the stands as the Leafs, Canadiens, or Oilers take the ice. They just want a high five or a stick. The kids in Thompson were doing that as well, but for Cliff and the Northstars. "The Northstars would walk up this long tunnel to the ice and it would just be full of kids asking for sticks," says Douglas. "'Can I get a stick? Can I have your stick after the game?'"

But Douglas had extra access to his hockey hero. "My sister was a year younger than Cliff so she would line up meet-and-greets with us and the players or get us a stick."

The Northstars beat the Yellowhead Chiefs to win the Manitoba Midget League title for the 1995–96 season. It was Cliff's last season with the team. He led them with 11 playoff goals and a team-high 13 assists for 24 points during that championship run. His father never missed a game. When the Northstars hit the road, Cliff Sr. did the same. It didn't matter how far: "I never missed any of his games," he says. The next year, when Cliff moved to Junior hockey, Cliff Sr. would have to drive a lot farther for home games.

In May 1996, the Manitoba Junior Hockey League announced they were heading north. Really north: an expansion team was granted to the Opaskwayak Cree Nation (OCN). OCN is an Indigenous community located directly across the Saskatchewan River from the town of The Pas. More than 6,500 people live in OCN; another 5,500 hundred live in The Pas. A six-and-a-half-hour drive north of Winnipeg, the team's owners decided the team would be called the OCN Blizzard. They were set to begin play on the OCN side of the river at the brand-new, 1,100-seat Gordon Lathlin Memorial Centre in fall 1996. It was a three-and-a-half-hour drive from Thompson. Now all the Blizzard needed were some players. And a coach.

Gardiner MacDougall is one of the winningest coaches in Canadian university hockey history. His University of New Brunswick Reds have won eight national titles. He also led the Saint John Sea Dogs to a Memorial Cup win when he served as the team's interim head coach in spring 2022. In spring 1996, he had just wrapped up his third straight season as a coach with the Lebret Eagles of the Saskatchewan Junior Hockey League. But MacDougall was not going back to Lebret. Despite a 37-25-2 record he was let go by Lebret in early May. A coach needs to coach, and when MacDougall got an offer, he took it. On May 24, 1996, MacDougall was hired as the first head coach and general manager of the OCN Blizzard. "The job started on June 1. The expansion draft was the next day," he remembers.

MacDougall had little to no time to put a team together, and he got to work. His office wasn't ready yet, so he set up shop in a room in the new arena. MacDougall may not have had a proper office, but he did know northern players. Aside from three years in Lebret, the transplanted Prince Edward Islander had spent time coaching with the Flin Flon Bombers. The north was now his home, and he knew all about Cliff Duchesne. In fact, he had him on his protected list when he was with Lebret. That meant that if Cliff was going to play Junior in Saskatchewan, it was Lebret or bust. "When I was with the Eagles, they had a fifty-man protected list. I had good contacts up in Thompson. I had four or five really good players from Thompson listed with me in Lebret. I would talk to them and say, 'You should think about the Saskatchewan Junior League. There are more scholarships out of Saskatchewan,'" says MacDougall.

That's what MacDougall would say when he was with the Eagles. Now he had a different message. "I just worked those guys, I talked to them all the time. I said, 'Listen, there's a change here. We're going to have our own team in the north.' And Cliff was a kid from the north in Norman with the Northstars who won Manitoba AAA the year before. He was a good player on the team."

The Blizzard wanted Cliff. But did young Cliff Duchesne want to go to the Blizzard? Like most skilled young players, Cliff had options. Lebret was still after him and the Brandon Wheat Kings, a Major Junior team in the WHL, were a possibility. On his way to Lebret, Cliff stopped in at The Pas and decided to check things out. The Blizzard had opened camp early. That's when some shrewd negotiations took place between young Cliff and MacDougall. Cliff was still thinking of Lebret and MacDougall realized that the kid was likely going to try his luck in the WHL. But if he was going to play Junior A, MacDougall wanted to make sure it was in The Pas with the OCN Blizzard.

"I told him, 'We'd like to keep you here. Before you go to your Major Junior camp tell me what will work to keep you here.' He was very direct: 'I need a new pair of shoulder pads.' I said, 'I'll tell you what. We'll go to the sport shop in The Pas. We'll go there tomorrow, and we'll pick whatever shoulder pads you want, and I'll get those shoulder pads for you and then you'll stay here and then go to Brandon.' He said, 'A deal's a deal.' I said, 'Okay, a pair of shoulder pads!'"

Gardiner still laughs about their negotiation all these years later. "Not sure we really had a deal," says the coach, "because he went to Brandon. But eventually he came back."

Like thousands of kids before him, Cliff Duchesne took his shot at Major Junior hockey. And like thousands of others, it didn't work out. Maybe it was his size—he was only 5'9"—maybe it was something else, but whatever it was, he found his way back to the Blizzard. He was about to start a beautiful relationship with the team, the town, and its people.

Things didn't get off to a smooth start. When Duchesne was released by the Wheat Kings, MacDougall told Cliff to drive his car to Dauphin, Manitoba. The Blizzard were on the road playing the Dauphin Kings. Cliff did what he was told. He hit the road and then hit the ice for his first game with the Blizzard. Then someone hit him: "He got in a fight [during the game] and the guy hit him and almost ruined Cliff's eye," says MacDougall. "I said, 'Listen, you can't drive your car.' I got the trainer to drive Cliff's car back."

Cliff Duchesne hopped on the team bus and nursed his eye all the way back to his new home. Apparently, he didn't do a really good job of it. Cliff didn't have a billet yet, so he spent the night, along with a few other players, in the basement of the head coach's house. The next morning, Gardiner's five-year-old daughter, Maddy, made her way to the basement, maybe to watch cartoons, maybe to just say hi to the players. The first person she saw was a battered teenage hockey player named Cliff Duchesne.

"She walks down the stairs and sees this guy! His eye just ballooned! She came up the stairs screaming. She hated hockey for about five years," Gardiner says, laughing. "Cliff didn't know what to do. He couldn't even play our opening game that weekend because of his eye. But he became a legend there."

The OCN Blizzard were not a typical expansion team: they were fantastic. Their gritty style immediately endeared them to people on both sides of the Saskatchewan River. Duchesne, his coach says, embodied everything about the northern community. "He was from the north and that's the image we wanted. We were going to be a hardworking team. I had no idea how we were going to do in that league."

This also wasn't a typical hockey community. The Pas, Manitoba, made national headlines in 1971 for the worst reasons. A nineteen-year-old Cree woman named Helen Betty Osborne was abducted while walking home late one night. She was studying to become a teacher. It was a case that exposed the racism young Indigenous people and women face. She was abducted by four men, sexually assaulted, and murdered. Only one man was convicted. An inquiry, held years later, found that racism and indifference toward Indigenous people played a role in Osborne's death. A memorial to her sits just outside The Pas.

"The death of Helen Betty Osborne really separated the reserve from the town," says MacDougall. "That lasted for years."

The Blizzard started winning. Along with the wins, they'd get those little confidence boosts that any team needs. One night that boost was provided by Cliff Duchesne. It is a moment that still sticks out for MacDougall. "We were on the penalty kill—tie game, late, and Cliff is on the three-on-five and he scored a short-handed goal. We were down a goal, or we tied it up, I think. He was on the ice, and he scored that goal. It was a big win for us. It was against a top team from Winnipeg. It was early in our first year.

"Cliff was just a really consistent player," MacDougall continues. "His work ethic was so contagious. Cliff wasn't the greatest passer. He didn't have the greatest shot, but he just worked so hard. He became a very tough forechecker and backchecker. If there was a forty-second shift, he was going to give you all forty seconds. He would be back in the zone, on the forecheck, power play, penalty kill—and he did it with the biggest smile. He was just excited."

In other words, Duchesne played the same way in The Pas as he did in Thompson. His father, just like before, never missed a game, driving all over the province to see his son play. "You want to know the truth? I was scared he was going to get hurt," says Cliff Sr.

Opponents of the Blizzard soon got a little scared of getting hurt, too. OCN became a rowdy place to play. MacDougall was used to rough-and-tough hockey from his time coaching in Flin Flon, and it appeared that people in The Pas liked their hockey rough, too. "When I started coaching in Flin Flon," says MacDougall, "they would tell me the stories of the old days of when Bobby Clarke and Reggie Leach played there. In those days opposing players sometimes came down with the 'Flin Flon flu.' In The Pas it became the OCN flu."

To make matters worse—or better, depending on whose side you were on—one year the team even added stands for the playoffs, cramming as many people into the rink as possible. "It was so full. It was kind of like the old Boston Garden," remembers the coach. "There was a big platform above the goal and seats over the opponent's bench. We were ruthless. The rink became even more intimidating for the playoffs. A great atmosphere to be a part of, especially our first year because it was all new."

On the phone, MacDougall tells me that Cliff and the Blizzard gave The Pas more than just a hockey team. It gave folks from both sides of the Saskatchewan River, OCN and the town of The Pas, something they could both get behind. "For all the fans up there, to have their own team—I could see the pride. Especially for the Indigenous people. They were so excited about their team. If we had success, you could just see it in their eyes. Their whole week would revolve around how the Blizzard did on Friday or Saturday night."

The Blizzard lost in the final their first year in the league. The eighteen-year-old rookie and his teammate Konrad McKay led the team with 81 points. In typical Cliff fashion, he also had 203 minutes in the box. He was turning a few heads. "The second year they couldn't do enough to get him to Brandon," says Cliff Sr. "But Cliff wanted to stay with Gardiner. He went back to The Pas." Major Junior hockey was calling for Cliff Duchesne, but he had found a home. "He loved The Pas, and they loved him."

"Cliff set standards for work ethic," says MacDougall. "There was a work ethic standard and there was a consistency standard. He was a leader. And because of the work ethic we had a real physical team, a fast team, and then it just became a really tough place for opponents to come up when they're coming to The Pas."

If Cliff sounds a lot like a Wendel Clark or a Bobby Clarke, there is more. He even had the look, the infamous "I'll do anything for the team" look that Clarke often wore. Cliff still had that contagious smile, although it did change one night. Cliff Sr., a man of few words, tells the story: "They were playing a team from Saskatchewan and a guy hit Clifford. Clifford was just skating. He didn't even do anything, and the guy hit him in the mouth with his stick."

Cliff Sr. is not a naïve man. He knows his son was likely up to something, trying to get an edge, tying to take his opponent off his game. Whatever it was that Cliff did or perhaps said, it worked: "I guess he couldn't take whatever Clifford was doing. My son just spit his teeth out—he never missed a shift. I looked down on the ice and Clifford looked up and he smiled at me."

Clifford Duchesne lost his teeth and the first thing he did was look up to the stands and smile at his father. He didn't look at the ref to make a call. He didn't growl or seek retaliation on his opponent. He smiled at his father, the one guy who never missed a game, because he was afraid his son would get hurt. Maybe that smile was Cliff's way of saying, "Don't worry, Dad, I'm all right." Maybe he was smiling because he had hit a rite of passage for any player: he lost his teeth.

"All he said was, 'Well, this stuff happens in hockey.' He just took every day the way it came," says Cliff Sr.

Gardiner MacDougall offers up this theory on the toothless grin: "His dad probably worshiped Bobby Clarke, another guy from the north. And Cliff probably thought, 'Now I'm a true hockey player.' He'd be banged up. I know one time his elbow was all swollen. But he'd never miss a game. He was a dream player for any coach."

"Gardiner knows him better than me," says Cliff Sr. "They were together all the time. He knows everything Cliffy done and how hard he worked. Cliffy, when he talked to me, he told me he thought a lot of Gardiner. I know Gardiner told me one time that the Blizzard were talking about trading Cliffy. He said, 'If they trade Cliff they might as well put me on the same bus.'"

———

Cliff and Gardiner spent three years together with the OCN Blizzard. Their final season in The Pas was a magical one. Twenty-year-old Cliff finished the year with 92 points in 66 games. But it wasn't his individual success that stood out. The Blizzard set a Manitoba Junior Hockey League record with 53 wins, 108 points, 29 home wins, and 24 road wins, and established another league record with 19 wins in a row. In a word: unstoppable. Cliff's MJHL career ended on a high, with a four-game sweep of the Winnipeg South Blues to win OCN's first MJHL title. The Blizzard took out the Winnipeg club 7–0 in the fourth and final game of the series in front of 1,607 fans at the University of Manitoba's Max Bell Centre. Cliff had two goals and an assist in the clinching game. "It's a beautiful ending," Cliff told the *Winnipeg Sun* after the game. "You can't ask for anything else but a championship. Now you just keep going."

Cliff and Konrad McKay were named co-MVPs of the playoffs. The Blizzard advanced to a best-of-seven against the champions from the Saskatchewan Junior League, the Estevan Bruins, for the ANAVET Cup. The winner would get a spot in the Royal Bank Cup Tournament to decide a national Junior A champion. The Blizzard took the first two games of the series but ended up losing in six games. The game six loss came in double overtime. Cliff's Junior career was over after three years with the Blizzard. "All three years," says MacDougall, "Cliff personified what our team was about, what the north was all about. 'Pride and the North' was our slogan.

"The first few years of that team connected everyone together because people had one common team," MacDougall continued. "We had big support from the Band. Hockey really brought the town and that reserve together, especially going to the finals the first year. We'd go on the road, and we would have such great support. Half of the crowd on the road would be Indigenous people from all over Manitoba. We were the pride and joy of all the Indigenous people from across Manitoba.

"Cliff just loved every part of the game and every part of the experience of The Pas. He enjoyed the billets. He enjoyed the parents of his teammates. Through Peewee, Bantam, and Midget he was the most popular guy on the team. He was a guy that everyone would want to see succeed."

Cliff didn't go on to a pro career, but he kept playing hockey. About a year after his final game with the Blizzard, he was named tournament MVP of the sixth annual Labatt's Rec Hockey Challenge in Shilo, Manitoba, in April 2000. He had two goals in the tournament final, a 5–2 win for The Pas Chiefs over the Winnipeg Stray Cats. Gardiner MacDougall had left OCN by then, too. He finished up a season as the Flin Flon Bombers' director of hockey operations that spring before becoming the head coach of the University of New Brunswick Reds for the following season.

That Christmas, just a year and a half after winning the Manitoba championship with Cliff and the Blizzard, MacDougall got the call that his hardworking star forward was gone. "It was my first year at UNB in Fredericton. We were having Christmas here, but I was going over to my mom's in PEI and I was just shattered that day. Cliff was just full of life. He lived 24/7. It was tragic because he was so vibrant, a kid, so full of life. If there was a chance [to survive] he was a kid that would, that's for sure."

The communities of Thompson, The Pas, OCN, northern Manitoba, and the entire Manitoba hockey family were devastated. Greg Douglas, the little kid who used to try to get Cliff's stick in his Northstars days, lost a hockey hero that day: "A good friend of mine, we used to call each other every Christmas morning to talk about what presents we got. I only would've been twelve or thirteen, something like that. He called me and let me know the news. I said, 'Holy smokes.' The town was pretty shook, for sure. It was crazy. You're only used to old people dying. Honestly, I don't even know how to answer how I felt."

Cliff's old coach with the Northstars, Doug Korman, gave the eulogy at the funeral. "I made mention that a lot of people, they need a team of horses to pull a team along. And we didn't. We just needed Cliffy."

Cliff was gone. But his body had still not been found. That spring, once things thawed a bit, the community got together and searched. "There were hundreds of volunteers," says the old coach, "and I was one of them, dragging the river for his body. That dragging went on for two or three weeks and finally we had to concede maybe we're not going to find him."

The official search for Cliff's body was called off. But his father never gave up. He kept searching. May turned into June. "And then I started to give up," says Cliff Sr. "But then I'd go out every second or third day. One Sunday I phoned my buddy. I said, 'Let's go for a ride.' We went out to the river, about maybe six or seven miles. We turned around and coming back there was a bay. There he was. In that bay he came up. He floated into that bay. He was waiting there for me when I come back."

Cliff Sr. had finally found his son, almost six months after the accident. For him, it meant everything. "I felt better. Before that, it was a pretty empty feeling."

Cliff Sr. had been told that if he found his son, he might not look too good; that the body, by that time, could be decayed. "But I looked at his face. It was perfect. The only thing, his one hand, there was a little bit of skin off of it because of the water. He was in good shape. I pulled him up and I put him on the shore."

"To this day," says coach Korman, "I haven't lost a child or nothing, but I can't imagine how Cliff still manages. It was a tough story, but it was a good one while young Cliff was here. If the kids I coach now could see what an example he was . . ."

In a way, the kids who play for the Norman Northstars and the OCN Blizzard carry on the Duchesne legacy. Douglas did just what his hockey hero did. He grew up to play Midget in his hometown of Thompson for the Northstars, and then went four hours away to play Junior in The Pas for the OCN Blizzard. "I was pretty proud to put on both of those jerseys. I grew up obsessed with the Northstars and going to every game," said Douglas. "To take the same path that Cliff took, I'm pretty proud to say I could do that. Not that I was a great hockey player or anything, but I'm just proud to say I got to play in the same places as a guy like Cliff."

Every year the Blizzard give out the Clifford Duchesne Hardest Working Player Award. And every year the Northstars do the same. Following Cliff's death, Doug Korman always made sure his Northstars teams made a stop whenever they rode through Bellsite, Manitoba, where Cliff Duchesne is buried. Greg Douglas was on one of those Korman-coached Northstars teams that would pull off the highway to pay their respects. So were countless other players. Year after year Korman and his team would stop at the grave. "Some of the players didn't maybe know Cliffy; they had heard of him, but they didn't know him. He is buried in a small community just off the highway. When we'd be traveling down that way, we'd make the bus driver go in. And we would all get off the bus. I would always leave something at the gravesite.

We would have a moment of silence and then I would tell stories about Cliff and what it meant to be a Northstar.

"I do it to this day: I still stop in there when I'm driving south and I'm on that side of the province. I will stop in there and say a couple of words and carry on," says Cliff's old Midget coach.

All these years later, Cliff is never far from Korman's mind: "I can just visualize how he looked at me. His smile. His work ethic. I could give him shit and he would not step back. He wouldn't pout. He would just work harder. He would turn it up a notch. People gravitated to him. Anybody who was around the rink or knew hockey, this was the kid. We knew he wasn't going to the NHL—God, he was five-nine, maybe five-ten—but we knew as a Junior hockey player he was going to have a career, and he did with OCN. He elevated his game, and he elevated the game of his teammates. He set the bar. For a coach, it's not very often you have a player like that. Once in a lifetime, maybe.

"It's kind of emotional thinking back about him. I always make an attempt, during Christmas, to drive down to the bridge, go to the gravesite, and pay respects, because I really thought of him as more than a hockey player. I thought of him as kind of like a son," says Korman.

Cliff Duchesne was just a kid when he died. But he was also just a kid when he filled two Manitoba communities with a pride that only an all-or-nothing hockey player can give a town. "Our game of hockey," says Gardiner, "has blue-collar roots, Canada-wide. A lot of times we think of the Sutters, all these families who were blue-collar people. Cliffy Duchesne was blue-collar. He employed every value of hockey and everything that you wanted a hockey player to be. It would've been his dream from six years old to play high-level hockey, to play Junior hockey.

He'd be the guy with the old wooden stick who would play on the pond for hours and would bring everything to the game. He would have that captive smile, even when he lost his teeth. There was that mischievous grin in his eyes. He would play every game like it was his last. He would practice every practice like it was his last. To me, he has the true value of a Canadian. The game is about the work ethic and getting better. And he would try to do that every time he showed up to the rink."

"He never quit," says Cliff Sr. "I don't know where he got the power from."

Cliff Duchesne with the Norman Northstars.

CHAPTER 11

Tyson Wuttunee

Kerrobert, Saskatchewan

When Tyson Wuttunee finally stopped playing in the Saskatchewan West Hockey League, he was forty-two years old. He spent the better part of two decades playing in the league and by the time he put a cap on his Senior hockey league odyssey, he had amassed 294 points in 197 games. But Tyson's story is not about numbers. His is not your typical Senior hockey story. Senior hockey is usually where a player finishes things up, and Tyson's story is not about an ending . . . it is all about beginning.

On the phone, he tells me, "I might as well tell you the whole story."

Tyson is like a lot of mid-forties guys in small-town Saskatchewan. He runs his own business—Ty's Excavating—and is a married father of three young girls. He has a son, Boston, a little older, a hockey player like his dad. He is a busy family man living a normal small-town life—the dream, many people might say. At one point in his life, the idea of living well in a small town was just that, a dream, and nothing more. Of his teenage years, Tyson says, "I had some parenting issues. I had no one really to look up to."

Life was pretty good for Tyson Wuttunee growing up in Saskatoon. He was like any other kid in town: he loved hockey. He played it all the time. He wanted to—planned to—play professionally. He would spend his days curving and cutting his sticks and would be on the ice as much as possible. However, everything changed when Tyson was twelve years old. His mother, Marcella, took a job in Montana. So, Tyson had a choice to make. He could move to Montana, where he wouldn't get a chance to play, or move to his dad's place on the Red Pheasant Cree Nation—"the rez," he called it. The rez was just outside North Battleford, Saskatchewan, far from Tyson's home in Saskatoon. "Playing minor hockey in Saskatoon was probably the best time of my life. I played with the Knights and the Barons," he says. Whatever decision Tyson made, his Saskatoon days were over.

In the end, Tyson moved to his dad's place. "Probably the worst mistake I've ever done in my career was moving up to Battleford," he muses. "I remember going out to try out for the Bantam AA team. I was coming from Saskatoon playing AA my whole life with guys who made the top and played in the NHL. I went to try out for their Bantam AA team, and I got cut. I ended up playing house league that year and I kind of got lost in the system."

The slick-skating kid who was a top player in Saskatoon couldn't make AA in North Battleford. That didn't make sense. Tyson tells me it might have been because of his last name: Wuttunee didn't mean anything special in Saskatoon, but in Battleford, the name came with a reputation. "It was kind of a bad name," Tyson says. "It was known as maybe a criminal name. I just couldn't get over why I didn't make the team that year. Now that I look back on it, it's a name that [maybe] some people [didn't like]. It was political. I was the best player on the team."

Tyson had the name, but he didn't fit the bill. He was new to Battleford, just a kid from the city who wanted to make the big team in his new town. "It was known as a badass name in Battleford, but I grew up with my mom in Saskatoon. I went to Catholic school and did everything right. And then she took a job in Montana. I had no choice, to continue playing hockey, I had to stay in Saskatchewan. I wasn't going to go move to Montana in the middle of nowhere. There was no hockey there. I just loved hockey, so I stayed. But I kind of got lost. And that was the biggest mistake of my career."

To some people, this might sound strange: Tyson was just an adolescent. But four decades later, he still feels strongly about that decision. He was lost in the hockey shuffle and he was lost in his new surroundings. He was a city kid on the rez: "I was fighting every day in school. I'm a white-complected Indigenous man."

It also didn't help that Tyson sported a haircut that wasn't all that cool with the other kids. Remember, he was twelve years old, and when you're that age and different in any sort of way, you stand out. He was coming from the city where boy band New Kids on the Block were all the rage. Alas for him, this haircut proved most unpopular in North Battleford: "I had a little tail in the back of my hair . . . that was the haircut. And I wore my hat up high. Every recess the fights were on. I was fighting and I ended up getting respect. It was a tough transition, for sure."

Soon enough, though, Tyson ditched the New Kids haircut. "I took the tail off and went with a little mullet in the back," he remembers. It was the perfect hockey hair. And even though he was only playing house league, that didn't kill Tyson's love of the game. If anything, the move to the rez only strengthened his resolve. He wasn't fitting in at school, he couldn't find a top-notch team to play on, but he could still play. Hockey was all he had. "I had hockey to fall back on. I kept to myself. I'd go skate after school. I'd do whatever I could to get on the ice," he says. "I just loved the game and being on the ice. Sometimes I was the only guy skating around. I remember going to the pond and making a rink because that's what we did as young boys in Saskatoon. We'd go to the pond and just play all day and all night long. I loved it. When I left Saskatoon, I lost all my friends that I grew up with. I lost all my close buddies."

But soon it was time to get out of hockey purgatory. A year on the pond, a year of (not) fitting in at school, and then a year of house league eventually coming to an end. "The following year I made Bantam AA. I didn't even have to try out. The coach just said, 'You're on the team.' I went to the camp. I didn't even play exhibition."

That year went well, and then like any other kid on a high-level Saskatchewan hockey path, Tyson wanted to make AAA Midget with the local team, the North Battleford North Stars. But he was cut. "I don't know why," he says. True to form, his AAA Midget dreams were not quashed: Tyson was offered a spot with the St. Michael's Thunder. They played two hours east, in Duck Lake. Even though that meant, just like a couple of years before, that Tyson would have to leave home again, he decided to give the Thunder a go: "We were stuck in the dorms there. I kind of got homesick and I said, 'I'm not doing this.' I went home and played Midget AA in Battleford. I tore it up. I won the scoring race and was MVP, but I was just getting lost in the tracks there."

Tyson was lost again. He had AAA Midget talent but he was not playing AAA Midget hockey. He was a Saskatoon kid who had tried life in North Battleford and then St. Michael's and it just wasn't working. Academics weren't top of mind—he struggled in school, yet hockey remained in the forefront, as it always did.

He thought, maybe he could try the Junior A route. The Humboldt Broncos were asking about him, and so were the Nipawin Hawks of the Saskatchewan Junior A League. "I actually went down to the Nipawin [rookie camp] and made the top two lines there," he says.

Tyson headed back to the rez after rookie camp and was soon invited back by the Hawks, this time to their main camp. He was good to go, but his father was not happy: "I remember almost getting into a scrap with my dad on the doorsteps of the house. He did not take me back to Nipawin's main camp. He said, 'No, we're not going.' I don't know why. I never did ask him after that. Maybe it was a money issue, but I would've made that team for sure. I was second on the list to go back and obviously you're going to make the team, but I ended up not going and I kind of spiraled downhill after that."

Tyson then did what a lot of teenagers did at that age. He got into alcohol. He partied a lot. He didn't seem to care about school, and now even hockey was almost marginal. Once upon a time he was a Midget AAA player who was not playing Midget AAA. Now he was a Junior A player not playing Junior A, so the next year he decided to give Junior A another shot. He had a friend who was playing for the Bonnyville Pontiacs in the Alberta Junior Hockey League. The team was holding open tryouts. Tyson hopped in his buddy's car and they headed west. "I made the team. I went there as a walk-on, and I made the team. I stuck there. I would've stayed but then again, I went downhill."

The problem for Tyson in Bonnyville was school. As in—he didn't go, and he was supposed to be completing grade twelve.

These were not the wild days of Junior A hockey. The coach, a former University of Alberta Golden Bear, just like the rest of the coaches in the league, stressed academics as well as hockey. That did not sit well with the young Saskatchewan sniper: "I ended up staying at my billets and chilling all day long. The coach came over one day, and I was home. He and a teacher came. They took me right [back] to school. They tried to get me in there [but] I just went back to my billets, and I said, 'No, I'm not going.' In the next couple days, I was gone. Back to the rez. Back with Dad."

Tyson hung out at home. His brother Sheldon was playing AAA Senior hockey for Battleford in the Wild Goose League. The "wild" in this particular Goose League was just enough to not care that a Junior-aged kid wasn't going to high school. Soon enough, Tyson was playing Senior hockey as a Junior-aged player. It went well: "I was kicking ass in that league. We were making a run for the AAA Allan Cup, but we ended up losing in the finals to the Lloydminster Border Kings that year. That was my nineteen-year-old year."

So now, Tyson was a Junior A player who was not playing Junior A; he was playing Senior AAA. The next season, by the time Tyson turned twenty, he was back playing Senior in Battleford. That's when opportunity came knocking again. His team hosted a Christmas tournament. It came with a twist, featuring Senior teams Battleford as well as Lloydminster, and college teams Lethbridge Pronghorns from the Canadian university ranks and Minot State from North Dakota. "I ended up having an unreal tournament."

Minot State liked what they saw and offered Tyson a scholarship. The Notre Dame Hounds from Wilcox, Saskatchewan, also liked what they saw and offered Tyson a spot on their Junior A team. Tyson, who fell off the hockey map when he left Saskatoon all those years ago, who couldn't stick in Junior, was now being offered a chance both to play at Minot State and to play for the Notre Dame Hounds, one of the most historic Junior A programs in the country. It had finally all come together: "I had it all lined up, but then I ended up getting a .08 at that time and I lost it all again."

Tyson was caught in Battleford driving under the influence. He did not go to Notre Dame, nor did he go to Minot State. He stayed at home. He had to pay a fine and do some community service. He could do one of two things: quit on life and himself, or keep going and keep doing what he loved. "It was tough, obviously. I had some parenting issues. I had no one really to look up to. I had abandonment issues from my childhood coming back. I just basically tried to stick with hockey. I fought through that .08 and kept playing. I just said keep it on the ice, play your ass off, get some goals, and I'll feel better about myself.

"That was my wake-up call."

Life was changing. The next year Tyson had a son, whom he named Boston Bird. He packed up his hockey bag and joined the Cut Knife Colts of the North Saskatchewan River Hockey League. He led his team in scoring and won league MVP. ("Now that you mention it . . . I never did get those trophies," he says with a laugh.) He played in the same league the following year. He was a Senior hockey player on the ice, but off the ice he was a young man looking for a home, looking for some kind of direction.

That summer was just like the rest, except for one day. Tyson was out "chasing cows" on the farm with his dad. These cows were owned by a man named Bill Flair. Flair knew of Tyson's hockey exploits, and he invited him to come play Senior hockey in a town called Kerrobert. Tyson was familiar with the team: the Kerrobert Tigers played in the Saskatchewan West Hockey League, and they had some pretty good players. He mulled over their offer and told Bill over supper, "Sure, I'll come." It was a simple yes, like the ones that he had given to teams before. But this time it was different. This yes would eventually give something Tyson he always wanted—a home. A family.

Kerrobert, Saskatchewan, is a little town of roughly one thousand people, located in west-central Saskatchewan, about 180 kilometres west of Saskatoon. It is conveniently located right where Highways 21, 31, and 51 meet. The town was named after a Canadian Pacific Railway executive, Robert Kerr, and was once known as the railway centre of west-central Saskatchewan. That's not the case anymore. Rail traffic was rerouted years ago. These days, Kerrobert is a centre for oil and gas workers, as well as farmers. The hockey team, the Tigers, traces its roots all the way back to the 1930s. "Tyson was a hot shot when he was younger. He was a super-skilled Native kid. They came out of there with heads as big as the world, because they were going to conquer the world," says longtime Kerrobert GM, coach, and former player Brad Murphy.

Tyson didn't exactly conquer the world when he showed up in Kerrobert, but he did make his presence felt in the west Saskatchewan Senior circuit. The points came easy, as they always did. He'd commute in from Saskatoon for games to play the role of local hero. He had 54 points in 21 games in his first season, followed by 53 in 24 games the following season. Tyson was finding a hockey home: "The league was really good, very competitive. The hockey was good. It felt good to come here. They welcomed you with open arms."

The league did come with its challenges in those early days.

"I was making a difference every night in small Saskatchewan west-central communities as an Indigenous person. You don't see that," Tyson says. "There were no Indigenous guys in the league except for me. I always wanted to compete. I wanted to show my style of play."

In other words, he was a high-flying, dynamic player. And he was Indigenous. That put a target on his back. These factors combined made for some miserable nights . . . he'd hear racist taunts from the crowd, sometimes more. "One night there were bottles thrown on the ice and people yelling, 'Hey, Wuttunee, did that [bottle] fall out of your pants?'"

For the most part, he would just put his head down and play. "It wasn't pretty, but that's the heart of the lion in me. I'll friggin' challenge anybody who wants to go on the ice. I'll score the big goal; I'll score that cheeky goal where no one can catch me. Maybe a toe drag. Whatever it took. Just showing my style."

But Tyson would still hear the taunts and the slights. One night he dropped the gloves on the ice and got in a fight. As he made his way off the ice, he heard "Go back to the rez!" from someone in the stands as he tried to make his way to his dressing room. Tyson wasn't going to ignore it. Not this time. He went right over to where the yell came from and confronted the crowd. "I said, 'Who said that?' It wasn't where I was going to kill somebody, but I wanted to confront them."

"Why would you say that to me? Why would you say such a thing?" That's what Tyson wanted to know from that fan. "I'd look at them and stare at them. I'd put them on the spot, as in, 'What are you doing, buddy?' And then everyone looks at him and he's the douchebag."

For the most part the catcalls only came from the stands, but one night an opposing player tried to target Tyson with the racist game. Chirping is one thing, comments like "Does your coach know you're on the ice?" or "I've seen more ice in my drink than you've seen tonight." Comments like that come with the territory. Racist taunts, however, are way over the line, and Tyson was absolutely not going to take it. "I remember one incident. I'm not going say the name of the town but one time a player on the other team said, 'Sober up!' I thought, 'That can't be right.' Who knows what it meant? I don't even care. It's just something that stuck in my mind over the years."

Tyson dropped the gloves. "I grabbed him, and he turtled [fell to the ice in a ball and covered his head]. I kind of attacked him. After that it was nothing but respect."

After three years in Kerrobert, Tyson Wuttunee was in his prime. He was living in Saskatoon, driving to games. The Kerrobert years were great; the team treated him like family, but Tyson was still in search of one off the ice. He was still playing the role of "Sasky Senior Import." If a call came in that was too good to turn down and he had to leave Kerrobert . . . and why not? He was single. He had no one to answer to but himself.

During that off-season, the phone rang: "The Luseland Mallards offered me unreal cash. They were in the same league and only ten minutes from Kerrobert." Tyson chased the money and joined the Mallards. They were loading up and were going to make a run for it. His season could not have started any better. He was scoring 5 or 6 points per game. In his first seven games with Luseland he put up close to 40 points. That caught the attention of a few folks outside Saskatchewan. After a hot start in Luseland, two more offers came in. The first one was from the Laredo Bucks of the Central Hockey League. It was professional hockey.

Sure, it wasn't the NHL, but it was a chance to venture outside his comfort zone and get paid to simply play hockey. Tyson was going to head to Texas. "I was really pumped. I was kind of on standby to go to Laredo. I was ready to fly out of Saskatoon."

But then the phone rang again and another offer came in, this one from the Laval Chiefs of the LNAH—the Ligue Nord-Américaine de Hockey. It was a league known for one thing: fighting. But beyond the fisticuffs it was a highly skilled league. There were two types of players in the LNAH: finesse players and fighters. Both sets of players basically kept to themselves. The players played and the fighters fought. "They were [also] offering up unreal money. The guy on the phone said, 'I got you a flight booked. I want you down here. I'll get you a thousand bucks a week to play in Laval. You'll be on the first line. You don't have to bring anything, just bring a bag. It's an ex–minor pro league. There's a bunch of ex-NHLers here.' So that decision was tough."

Tyson mulled it over. He chose the thousand dollars a week from the Laval Chiefs. Luseland offered big bucks to leave Kerrobert, but his mind was made up.

"It was the wrong decision," Tyson says. He knew it almost immediately after his feet left Saskatchewan soil. "I ended up jumping on a plane that night and I flew to frickin' Laval. I remember sitting on the plane shaking because I knew what the hell this league was about with the fighting."

Things went well when Tyson first arrived in Laval. The team, as promised, fit him out with brand-new gear, and they set him up in an apartment. The Chiefs played in the Colisée de Laval, the same rink where Mario Lemieux once played Junior hockey. The Chiefs had high hopes for their newest player: "I had Mario Lemieux's old stall in the dressing room."

Just like when he moved to the rez as a kid, he was once again in a whole new atmosphere. It was all French, foreign to the kid from Saskatoon: "I remember thinking, 'Oh my God, what am I doing here?'

"The hockey was all pro. A pro atmosphere. The top six players were all scorers. They played hockey. They played really good hockey. Plus, the goons. They kept to themselves. They just kind of dressed up and did their thing. They had [the fights] lined up before the game. 'This is who's going, this is who is fighting who.' The guys who were there to do the finesse part, we just sat on the bench and waited until they were done fighting and then boom, we went and played hockey."

Tyson didn't stick around long. He only played in four games with the Laval Chiefs. That warning shot with the .08 a few years back stuck in his mind and he didn't like what was going on around him: "It was just different. It was partying. It was just too much," he says. "One night after a game we went out to a club in Montreal. There was some kind of gang thing there, a couple of murders. We got stuck in that bar until six am for questioning and they wouldn't let us go. I just said, 'I'm going home.' I took all my shit and flew home the next day. I just couldn't take it out there."

That was the end of the Quebec experiment. It was back to Saskatchewan. But it wasn't back to Kerrobert. Tyson spent the next few years going back to the role of single hockey nomad. He played in Kerrobert, Eston, Portage College, Biggar, and as always, in Native tournaments around the province.

The Native tournaments were a point of pride for Tyson. They would take place on weekends, mainly in the spring, after the Senior season closed, and big cash would be up for grabs. It was community against community, with a few imports allowed for each side. If you walked into an Indigenous tournament and saw it for the first time, you would be stunned by the high quality of play. Or to be more precise, "Minds would be blown," Tyson tells me. "When you watch Europeans play on TV, that's the kind of calibre First Nations players are. They're all hands and finesse. There's some good fights and good tussles, too."

Calvin Sapp, better known as Sappy, is a fixture at these tournaments throughout Saskatchewan. He spends his weekends as a trainer: he has been a trainer for more than forty years, both for Allan Cup teams and for Junior teams. He ended up sharing a dressing room with Tyson at Native tournaments for over a decade. He can't stress enough just how talented the kid who went from team to team all over Saskatchewan was: "Where does he rate from all the players I've seen? I would say the top five, easy. And I know my hockey players. He rates right up to the top. I look back on Tyson, and I think, 'Why didn't he go play in the States with the amount of talent he had?'"

"All the big tournaments worked out awesome," says Tyson. He'd make some good money, play some good hockey, and connect with other Indigenous players. "You feel at home. Everyone is respectful. The First Nations people don't hold grudges, not being in the community or being away for so long. When you come back, they're going to welcome you."

From team to team, town to town, the hockey, as always, was great. But there was something missing. Tyson knew what it was. He had a family on the ice and in the dressing room. But he did not have a traditional family away from the rink. He had a son, Boston Bird, who was growing up, but Tyson didn't really have anyone outside his hockey life that he could lean on. That is what he always wanted. One night, finally, things came together for the kid who had had to leave his mom to live on the rez when he was only twelve years old. Fittingly, he met his wife through hockey. "She saw me play a few games—I met her after one of the games and we totally fell for each other."

Robbi Phillips, a schoolteacher, was a local girl from the Kerrobert area. They started dating in 2009 and eventually married. They now have three daughters. "Obviously I had some childhood problems and issues. [Robbi] came from a family that had a mom and dad and brothers and sisters. She had the foundation to make a family that I've always wanted. All my buddies had that life, and I never had that life. That's what kept me going and still keeps me going. I want to give my kids the life I never had, for the parents to be there and be supportive for anything that they want to do. To give them that opportunity to have Mom and Dad in the house. That's what keeps me going."

Tyson's vagabond hockey days soon came to an end. There were no more commutes from Saskatoon to wherever. Kerrobert became both Tyson's on-ice and off-ice home. He played his last six Senior seasons for the Tigers. In total, Tyson ended up playing Senior hockey for more than two decades . . . which never happens. But Tyson Wuttunee did. "It was kind of my job over twenty years on the weekends. I made some good money playing hockey in Saskatchewan for these little teams. I was the name. And it was fun, the road trips, the beers after. We'd go to a bar after just to hang out.

"I would always look forward to Friday night. Two o'clock in the afternoon would come and I'd have a pregame meal. Senior hockey was a big deal in Saskatchewan. Going for a pregame meal—or to a movie with the boys—and hanging out and going out that night and scoring a nice goal or getting that nice assist. I cherish those moments today and I will never forget them."

Tyson knew his days on the Senior circuit were ending. He was forty-two, and things were changing. His teammates were getting younger. It was getting "weird" in the dressing room . . . as in, there was no more Metallica or AC/DC playing over the speakers. The kids were listening to techno. Now there was endless pregame stretching. Tyson was more of a get-up-and-go kind of guy. The new guys were slick and clean-shaven, dressed up. Tyson preferred his tracksuit.

Even on the ice things changed: Tyson went from high-scoring wizard forward to defenceman for his last few years. "During the end I slowed him down a little bit," says his old coach Brad Murphy. "I basically told him that he wasn't going to score twenty goals again and I made a defenceman out of him. It wasn't the first thing he wanted to do, I'll tell you that. But he enjoyed playing the last four or five years. Guys who have that sort of skill set—you can turn them into a defenceman in two weeks."

Tyson kept playing in Native tournaments as well. The biggest one of all is the Fred Sasakamoose "Chief Thunderstick" National Hockey Championship, an invitational tournament hosted every spring in Saskatoon, named after Sasakamoose, the first Treaty Indigenous player in the NHL. It is community against community. "It is everything," Tyson says. "It is our NHL. Our Stanley Cup. Freddy paved the way for our people. The people put so much work into that tournament. It's big . . . something all these First Nations kids look forward to. And pro guys come back to play in it, or guys like myself who have played Senior hockey. We are looking to help the next generation. That tournament is everything. Kids are asking for sticks after the games. The stands are packed. It is beautiful to see."

Tyson was the tournament's first-ever MVP, having won the Thunderstick three times. In his final tournament he got to play on a line with his son, Boston. "It was the best feeling. Boston sat beside me. Obviously, you gotta get paid to play and I paid Boston out of my pocket to help him out. He loved it. To have him sit beside me and play centre beside me in my last tournament—it was awesome. For me to say to him, 'Go take the draw, son,' was the best thing."

The Kerrobert Tigers said goodbye to Tyson Wuttunee in his final home game on February 12, 2022. Tyson knew what was coming. The team's executives told Tyson they were going to have a night for him. "I kind of got the word that they were going to hang my jersey."

Tyson had his family on the ice with him. The kid who came to Kerrobert, alone, just to play, was now a family man, standing on the ice with his wife and three daughters, watching his number 71 being retired in this small Saskatchewan town. "It warms my heart. I look at these kids now, when you walk in the rink, and they say, 'Holy shit, it's Tyson Wuttunee.' It's awesome. I know I could've gone somewhere. I could've played somewhere else. I could've done this and that, but honestly, I wouldn't change it. Not leaving Saskatchewan and playing here and making this league better and being a pioneer, now looking at these kids that are coming up and the respect that they give me when I walk into the rink . . . it's the best feeling in the world."

But it wasn't a one-way exchange that night in Kerrobert. This town had welcomed him all those years ago. "In our culture, the blanket is a signature of showing respect, [of] bringing someone into the family. I made my mom purchase two Pendleton blankets. When I married my wife, my family wrapped her in a blanket to accept her into our family. So that blanket means a lot to us. I gifted a blanket to the team because they took me in as family, into the hockey team and the community, and they gifted me back with one."

Most of the time Senior hockey is the end; but sometimes it is the beginning.

"It gave me a life that I would've never had. I always tell my wife, 'If I had made the NHL, I never would have met you, and we'd never have this life.' I'm grateful every day."

Tyson Wuttunee on the night he was
honoured by the Kerrobert Tigers.

CHAPTER 12

Randy Keller

Claresholm, Alberta

Hope. You have to have it if you want your dream to become true. You can dream all you want, but without hope, there's no chance you will ever turn that dream into reality.

Claresholm is about as Alberta as you can get. The town of just under four thousand sits pretty much halfway between Calgary and Lethbridge along Highway 2, a little closer to Lethbridge to the south than Calgary to the north. The town is surrounded by ranchland and has produced its fair share of rodeo stars, including Jill Besplug, who won two straight barrel racing titles at the Calgary Stampede in the early 2000s. The town has produced other stars, like Louise Crummy McKinney, the first woman elected to a legislature in Canada. She was the member of the Legislative Assembly of Alberta for Claresholm from 1917 to 1921. But as honourable and historic as that is, most kids across Canada don't dream about growing up to become politicians. Many dream about hockey and Claresholm was no exception.

The town has never produced a player that has made it all the way to the NHL, but Claresholm does have its own hockey heroes. And at least one of them gave every young player in town something special in the late 1980s: hope. "Randy Keller was the first hockey hero I had growing up in the eighties," says Yellowknife, Northwest Territories, elementary school principal Landon Kowalzik.

Kowalzik, or Mr. K as he is known to his young students, is the type of guy who just loves the game. When *Hockey Day in Canada*, a day-long celebration of hockey on Sportsnet, made its way to Yellowknife back in 2019, Kowalzik went out of his way to make the event as special as he could for his students. They were decked out in hockey jerseys and got to host the Sportsnet crew, as well as several NHL alumni, at their school. You could see the pride on Mr. K's face.

But long before he was a principal "up north," he was a hockey fan "down south." He was a very typical eight-year-old kid in Claresholm, looking for something or someone to grasp on to in the hockey world: "I didn't have a favourite team initially. I would watch hockey with my dad. My dad started cheering for the Oilers. He was originally a Leafs fan, but he started cheering for the Oilers, so I started to watch, too. I didn't watch enough because the Oilers were only on TV once a week. To be honest, I didn't really have a favourite player. Randy was my first favourite player because I could connect to him."

Randy Keller was a big deal in Claresholm. Landon first got to see him, up close, one night in Lethbridge. He and a bunch of his minor hockey teammates, along with their parents, headed down Highway 2 to Lethbridge. But Landon and his buddies weren't cutting across cattle country—an hour's drive—to see the Hurricanes. And they weren't making the drive to Lethbridge to see the Moose Jaw Warriors. They were going to see Claresholm's hockey hero, Randy Keller.

Keller was a twenty-year-old centre for the Warriors, producing about a point a game for Moose Jaw. Kowalzik had read and heard much about Keller, but he had never seen him. That changed that night when he and a mob of Claresholm kids hit Lethbridge: "A whole bunch of minor hockey teams from Claresholm went to Lethbridge to watch the Hurricanes and Warriors play. Most of us didn't actually know Randy because he had been gone for years. We had seats behind the Moose Jaw bench that night. We had a whole bunch of kids, from seven to eleven years old, all of us yelling, 'We want Randy! We want Randy!'"

Landon was an eight-year-old kid cheering for a twenty-year-old kid. But at that young age, twenty might as well be forty—Keller was a man in his eyes. And Keller gave them a gift just by being on the ice that night. The gift of hope.

"It was supercool because we didn't know anybody else who had gone that far in hockey. It gave us somebody in the sport about whom we could tangibly say, 'Hey, that could be me.' Especially because he wasn't a big guy. Randy was listed at five ten. He was probably five nine. And here he was playing in the WHL against guys who you knew were going to play in the NHL the next year. It made you think—there's a chance that maybe someday that could be me. A bunch of us kids felt that way. Yeah, it was cool. We had fun because we got to go to a hockey game in the Dub [the WHL], which we didn't normally get to do; it made you feel like that dream is possible. It's not quite so unreachable."

Then, just like that, at least to young Landon Kowalzik, Keller disappeared. "He really was a mystery to me."

He didn't see Keller play again for years. That's because Keller was on the type of journey familiar to thousands of young aspiring hockey players before him. If he was going to make it, he had to leave town. Keller had, in fact, first left Claresholm a few years before young Landon saw him that night in Lethbridge.

Forty years ago, Randy was so good that he and two other kids from his Bantam team got an invite to the Fort McMurray Oil Barons rookie camp. The drive to rookie camp wasn't so bad, just an hour and a half west to Crowsnest Pass, so Randy gave it a go. He put on a good enough show to get an invite to the Oil Barons' main camp. Randy had never been north of Edmonton, and that was a hell of a long way. But if you're going to make it, you have to hit the road at some point. Randy and his parents hopped in the car and started the eight-and-a-half-hour journey north to Fort Mac. They were leaving ranchland and heading to the oil sands. Randy felt lost: "We ended up on Highway 63, a two-lane highway in the middle of nowhere. I didn't really know where I was going until I got there."

The highway to Fort Mac wasn't even twinned until 2016. It was littered with trucks making their way north. But they got there and after a good camp, Randy made the team. He was fifteen years old, playing in the rough-and-tough Alberta Junior Hockey League. His mother and father headed back down to Claresholm, but luckily for Randy, he had family in his new town to help with the transition. "I was fortunate. My dad's older sister was living up there at the time so that made it a lot easier. I lived with them for the first two years."

Fort McMurray was tough country and the AJHL in the mid-1980s was just as tough. The trips for the Oil Barons were long ones: the closest teams in the North Division were the Sherwood Park Crusaders, St. Albert Saints, and Fort Saskatchewan Traders. Each one of those teams is in the Edmonton area and rivalries were fierce. Brian Shantz was a local kid from Fort Mac who played on a line with Randy. Before the two ever skated together, Randy got a call from Shantz: "He tells me, 'I got called up when I was fifteen. The first game I played was in Sherwood Park. The boys are putting Vaseline on their face before warm-ups because they plan on starting a brawl.' And I thought, 'Geez, what are we getting into?'"

That first year, the goals and assists didn't come easy on the ice. However, Randy did put up some decent numbers for a kid who was playing against nineteen- and twenty-year-old young men: 8 goals and 16 assists in 51 games. A couple of years later, the kid from Claresholm was an "AJ" superstar. By then Brian Shantz and Randy were on the same line. "I called him 'Tex'—we all called him that. I guess because he's from Claresholm and in Fort McMurray we consider that a country boy," says Shantz.

Tex, Brian, and another hometown kid from Fort McMurray, Trevor Buchanan, formed the top line for the Oil Barons in 1987–88. That year Randy Keller did what no other Fort McMurray Oil Baron had ever done before: he scored 64 goals in a single season. It is an Oil Barons record that still stands today. "Humble" is how Keller is often described by his old teammates, so we'll let Shantz detail how his linemate did it: "He could score from anywhere. He could come down the wall and beat you with a slapshot. He could beat you in tight with his hands. Anytime anyone scores 64 goals they know what they're doing. He was very talented of course, but he wasn't one of those lazy guys who try to get by on natural talent. The majority of his points and goals came from working hard, grinding. He didn't go end to end, per se, and feed everybody. It was just a combination of everything that he had. He worked hard and went to the dirty areas to score a lot of goals. Some guys are blessed with only a shot or tremendous hands. He kind of had it all. But he had to work hard to get to certain areas to score his goals."

A seventeen-year-old kid named Cam Moon was a goalie on that Oil Barons team for the first half of the season. If there is a guy who knows western Canadian Junior hockey, it is Cam Moon. He played in the AJ, he played in the Dub, and he spent two decades as the play-by-play announcer for the Red Deer Rebels before becoming the radio play-by-play voice for the Edmonton Oilers. When Moon played for the Oil Barons, he knew he was watching something special. "Randy's compete level, if you want to use a phrase from today, was so high," begins Moon. "He really battled. There was something about the way he played. He played so hard that he made you want to play that hard. He was inspirational. I was a young seventeen-year-old rookie, and my eyes are wide open, and I see a guy like Randy Keller who had been in the league for a while—in my eyes he was very worldly. He played so hard and had a lot of great leadership skills. For sure he was one of the best players not just on the team but in the league. He was an elite player in the Alberta Junior Hockey League. A real quality guy, easy to talk to. Absolutely down-to-earth and certainly was one of the key cogs on the team."

That season didn't end well for the Fort McMurray Oil Barons, but it did end well for Keller. If you're a good enough hockey player, when one door closes, another opens, even a little. Keller was going to the WHL. The Kamloops Blazers called him up for the playoffs. Then that small opening widened up when an injury took down another Blazer. "At the start in the WHL," says Randy, "I felt that I really maybe didn't belong there at some practices. As the first playoff rounds went on, I started to feel a little more comfortable in that setting. Mike Needham blew his knee out. I ended up getting put up on the first line with Mark Recchi and things just seemed to fall into place on that playoff run."

That last name might ring a bell: Recchi had 1,533 points in his NHL career and is in the Hockey Hall of Fame. That winter Recchi led the Blazers with 154 points. The AJHL superstar was getting a chance to play with a WHL superstar: "It was awesome," says Randy. "When I tell the young kids around here that I had a chance to play with a guy with an outstanding NHL career like that, believe me, they are all ears. All you had to do was get to the spots and he would find you. I didn't have great numbers on that playoff run but I put up a few so that part went all right. You found the spots and the puck would be there. You knew where you had to go. Plus, Mark was a great shooter himself. I think that's why the Penguins ended up taking him, because he could read the ice so well."

Randy played in eighteen playoff games with the Blazers that spring. He ended up with 4 goals and 4 assists. The Blazers lost to Trevor Linden and the Medicine Hat Tigers in the WHL Finals, four games to two. The next season, Mark Recchi played 15 games with the Pittsburgh Penguins and Trevor Linden scored 30 goals for the Vancouver Canucks. And Randy Keller's days in Fort Mac were over. He was a full-time WHLer.

He started the year in Kamloops and then joined Moose Jaw, and that's when Landon Kowalzik saw him play the Hurricanes in Lethbridge. And yes, he can remember the Claresholm kids cheering for him whenever he'd play there. "Some of the younger kids, some of the Atom- and Peewee-age kids, would be there. They would ask you to sign autographs and stuff. I thought that was pretty cool being twenty, just showing that it can be done."

Kowalzik may have thought that Keller disappeared after

that night in Lethbridge; but he didn't. He finished the season in Moose Jaw. In his one and only complete season in the WHL, he had 59 points in 67 games and 1 goal in 7 playoff games. Then he went home, at least for a couple of months. "I was just working at the local golf course."

Landon wasn't a golfer, which meant he didn't see Randy there. He didn't see him when he kept playing hockey. After the Dub, Randy headed north again, this time to Calgary, where he played three years of college hockey. First a season with the Mount Royal Cougars and then two with the Southern Alberta Institute of Technology (SAIT) Trojans. In his third and final season, he led the Trojans in scoring. Once in a while the Trojans would play the Northern Alberta Institute of Technology (NAIT) Ooks and his old Oil Barons teammate Cam Moon: "I remember playing at NAIT and he was playing for SAIT. I remember thinking, 'Hey, there's Randy Keller.' And of course, he was one of their best players."

With his college career behind him, Keller decided to give the pros a shot. It was goodbye Calgary, and hello Louisville, Kentucky. His stay did not last long. "They were the Icehawks, back down in the East Coast Hockey League. I went for six weeks. I don't know, I just woke up one day and I thought, 'You know what? I just don't see myself riding the buses. I don't think I'm going to go anywhere with the game.' And I just ended up coming back and working and I've been here ever since."

Life had taken Keller right back to where he started, to his hometown of Claresholm. But his legend was only just beginning. Randy and his brother Blaine had played together at SAIT. Blaine beat Randy back home by a year. In fall 1991, Blaine and a buddy got together and established a Senior team, the

Claresholm Thunder. The team played in the aptly named Ranchland Senior Hockey League. The next fall, with six weeks in Louisville behind him, Randy Keller wasn't ready to totally pack it in. He went from AJ superstar to Ranchland superstar: "The last time I played in Claresholm I was fifteen," says Randy, "and now I was twenty-four. Our team was pretty good, when you think about it. We had a few kids besides myself who had played Junior hockey at one level or another, in the AJ or the Dub. Our team just sort of took off."

Claresholm was officially thunderstruck. Among the fans was a soon-to-be thirteen-year-old Landon Kowalzik: "At the beginning a few people came to the games but by the end of the regular season and the playoffs it was absolutely packed. It was a typical small-town arena. There is only seating on one side and by the playoffs it was absolutely packed, standing room only. And it was mostly thanks to Randy. He was the best player on the team."

The man who had once given the town hope was now giving something else: entertainment and pride. I ask Landon to give me some idea of what the Thunder meant to him. "How do you describe it? In some sense, I don't know if it's typical for all small towns, but there wasn't often a whole lot to be proud of because there's not much there. So being able to have the team itself was fine, but the fact that there was somebody on the team who was so good, it made me, as a person growing up in the town, proud. And being a hockey player from that same town, you almost felt part of it. He was a hometown boy who made it to a higher level than any of us ever had or anyone else from the town had, and he came back. When he came back, we thought, 'Okay, he's coming back to our town. So, our town is special. It's important. It's worthwhile.' All those things. It brought a renewed sense of community to the town because that was the place for everybody—and I mean everybody would go to the arena on a Friday night. You'd have five-, six-year-old kids, all the way up to seniors. Everyone would come together. It was all about that one team. And we were the best that year. And it wasn't because we brought in players from outside, which later with the progression of the team we had to for sure, but in 1992–93 the biggest star, hands down, was our own Randy Keller."

Keller and the Thunder took on the best the Ranchland Senior Hockey League had to offer. They'd hit the road for games against teams like the High River Flyers or Fort Macleod. But no matter what week it was, the Thunder would always be back home in Claresholm, to put on a show on a Friday night. "The arena was the place to be on Friday nights," says Randy. "I know for a lot of people they wanted a night out, because there isn't much to do. We don't have a movie theatre or anything like that. Friday-night entertainment was the Senior Thunder, and we had a good team, so the product was good. In the playoffs this rink was rafter to rafter. It was good to see. You just don't see that anymore."

The Thunder won the Ranchland championship in Randy's first year with the team. They became a mainstay in Claresholm throughout the 1990s. Randy got older and kept playing. Fans got older, too, like Landon Kowalzik, who soon discovered that like every other Senior hockey team on the planet, the Thunder liked to keep the party going after a Friday-night win—or loss. "The goal song of the Thunder was 'Thunderstruck.' Of course, that also became the bar song. After I graduated high school the place to go to was Douros. It was the lounge in town that everybody went to. They were always playing that song. After the games it was a party. Randy and the team, they were beloved. It stayed that way for years and years. It was the one thing that we really had in our small town. He gave life to the town."

"*Meaning* would probably be the right word," Randy says, when I ask him what the Thunder gave to his hometown. "Not only to the people from town, but people from the towns around us knew that we had a pretty good Senior team. Even some of them would venture in to watch us on Friday night. A lot of my buddies who I grew up with didn't play the sport, but they were here cheering for us all the time. It was just a way to get together."

Like most things in a small town, nothing gold can stay. By the time Randy was in his mid-thirties, the Thunder had folded. He went down the road to Fort Macleod and played for a few more years, and finally quit playing when he was thirty-seven. But there was a brief comeback. "I did play one year, when I was forty," he laughs. "Fort Macleod asked me if I could come back for one more season. The funny thing about that season was that the two kids I played with on my line were Claresholm kids. Their ages added together didn't add up to mine. I was like the grandpa out there, the Gordie Howe."

Claresholm was the perfect town to grow up in playing hockey, and still is. The Claresholm Arena has always had an open-door policy. "Every time you wanted to get on the ice you could go out on the ice and skate. Our arena is open all day long for the kids to take advantage of it. They are always down here," says Randy Keller over the phone. He now works for the town.

"I'm actually in the rink right now," he says. "The front doors are open. There's nobody in here, but if somebody was to come in the door, they could put the skates on and go for a skate."

The once-full arena, packed every Friday night, isn't so packed anymore. When Randy grew up in Claresholm the sporting schedule was pretty straightforward: "In winter, you played hockey. In summer, you played baseball. But I find now as time moves on . . . in some of these small towns, hockey's dying a little bit."

Kids have options now. The city doesn't seem so far away anymore. And let's face it, hockey isn't cheap, even in a place like Claresholm, where you can hop on the ice free of charge. But one thing you can't take away are memories, hope, and pride. That's what Randy Keller gave Claresholm, or at least that's what he gave to a kid who grew up in Claresholm, who is now a forty-something educator in Yellowknife. "Aside from being a hero for so many people," says Kowalzik, "and for a humble guy who doesn't go out of his way to get attention, he is still loved by hundreds of people in Claresholm—in fact, thousands of people in Claresholm, who saw him throughout his career."

If you're ever in town and would like to see Randy's stats, you can find them at the arena in Claresholm. His old Fort McMurray Oil Barons sweater is framed and hangs in the lobby of the arena. The display comes complete with Randy's career stats, whether they were from Claresholm, Fort Mac, Kamloops, or Moose Jaw. Proof that he never really disappeared after all: "I see my jersey every time I head into the lobby, and every once in a while I'll go over to read the write-up. Just read it and reminisce a little bit, and continue on.

"I think I had a good career. As a kid you always dream about getting to the NHL. I have nothing to hang my head about. I left at fifteen, worked hard for eight years. Maybe I could've pursued the dream a little longer, riding the buses and stuff, but ultimately, I thought, 'This isn't my dream. Why not come back home and start a life?' People ask me questions about hockey. You try to answer them in the right way. You try to give some kids hope. Even now the younger ones don't know me, but their parents do. You try to answer questions for them and help them out if they pursue the game. I always try to help them out."

Randy Keller stands in front of the display honouring his career in his hometown rink in Claresholm, Alberta.

CHAPTER 13

Richie Perreault

St. Albert, Alberta

"**A**s kids it was a big deal for us to go down to a St. Albert Comets game. There was only one rink in town. If you could manage to get down to a Comets game that was a really big deal. And the guy on the team that everybody idolized was Richie Perreault," says Troy Murray.

Troy Murray was one of the first players to come out of the St. Albert minor hockey system and make it all the way to the NHL. He grew up playing minor hockey at the same rink where the St. Albert Comets, a Senior team of the Edmonton Central Hockey League, played. Murray eventually ended up playing Junior A for the St. Albert Saints of the Alberta Junior Hockey League. After a 100-point season with the Saints he left for the University of North Dakota for two seasons. Then Murray made the Chicago Blackhawks. He ultimately played 914 NHL regular season games for the Blackhawks, Jets, Senators, Penguins, and Avalanche. Murray has won World Junior gold, scored 99 points in a single NHL season, and at one time or another he could call Denis Savard, Chris Chelios, Jaromir Jagr, Ron Francis, Peter Forsberg, and Joe Sakic teammates. And he still remembers a guy named Richie Perreault.

"I was actually talking to a friend of mine recently and he remembered the same thing about going to the Comets games," Murray says. "You'd scrape up a couple bucks and you'd go down there. That was a big deal back then. And like I say, Richie, he was *the* guy on that team.

"We thought, 'Those guys are men! And this hockey is amazing!' We didn't know any better because the Comets were the biggest game in town. And when the Comets were playing the place was packed."

St. Albert was a town of about 15,000 in the mid-1970s when Richie Perreault and the Comets were the main draw. "We barely went into Edmonton. Our little rink in St. Albert was the place to be," says Murray.

Why would a kid want to leave St. Albert, then? You could watch your hockey heroes at the rink and see them around town if you were lucky. "It was so different back then," says Murray. "Richie was working for the city. You'd see him in his white overalls working, and then you'd see him on the Comets and you'd think, 'Wow, this is pretty cool.'"

If the fire marshal wasn't looking, the St. Albert Arena could hold up to eight hundred fans, maybe a few more. Those seemed like huge crowds to kids like Murray and his buddies, but Perreault had played in front of larger ones. And he'd passed on a chance to play in front of thousands more. The thought of Perreault going pro? It never occurred to a young Murray: "I don't even know how old Richie would have been when he played for the Comets. Twenty-five? Thirty? I think that he was just happy with his life and what he had. And playing for the Comets was good enough for him."

About fifteen years before Troy Murray started his minor

hockey career in St. Albert, Perreault was on the ice as much, if not more, than any kid in town. If there was a frozen outdoor rink in town, he was on it. Like a lot of kids at the time, Richie didn't grow up wealthy. He didn't get his first brand-new pair of skates until he was eleven years old: "They might have been Tacks," Perreault recalls, thinking of the legendary CCM skates that every Canadian kid wanted at one time or another.

Richie had a love of hockey in common with most of the kids at his school. There was one thing different about him: he was Indigenous. He lived in the city and his mother and father spoke Cree. Richie, like a lot of other Indigenous kids, put up with name-calling and bullying. Hockey and sports, though, seemed to be the great equalizer for him. Richie was a great young hockey player. That ability made him just one of the kids out on the ice. He kept skating on the frozen rinks, kept playing. By the time he was in Midget and Juvenile, he was playing for two teams a season. He got really good, attracting the attention of scouts from what was then called the Canadian Major Junior Hockey League. We know it now as the Western Hockey League, but whatever the name, it was the best Junior league in the west.

Richie passed up an offer from the nearby Edmonton Oil Kings and settled on the Moose Jaw Canucks. He got a little homesick his first year in the league and spent some time playing in Calgary. For most of his two seasons in the western league, Richie played for head coach Brian Shaw and the Moose Jaw Canucks. Richie was a big kid. He could skate. He could shoot. He could hit. He could also accept reality: "I was a fighter. That's what I was brought down to Moose Jaw for, to protect some of the guys," says the affable seventy-five-year-old, from his home in St. Albert.

The bus rides were long, but "[w]e used to play cards to pass the time. It didn't seem that long." Trips back to Edmonton to play the Oil Kings had a bonus. Richie's biggest fan, his mother, Aileen, and dozens of other friends and family would always watch those games. The hockey was top-notch. Richie was just a kid but playing against other kids who would soon go on to be household NHL names.

"I got to play against some really, really good hockey players. I thought Bob Clarke was the best in our league at that time," says Perreault. "Bobby Clarke was like a [Mark] Messier. He would stick you if the time came and you knew that. I know if I ran him in the corner he'd get up and skate all the harder. I was always really impressed with the way he played his game."

Clarke was the leader of the Flin Flon Bombers. He had a sniper of a right-winger at his side, named Reggie Leach, who would go on to score 61 goals in a single NHL season and become a fixture alongside Clarke a few years later with the Broad Street Bullies, the Philadelphia Flyers. "I remember hitting Reggie one time into the boards. It was a real good check. He sort of stayed away from me after that."

In the NHL the Flyers made the "Philly flu" famous. When it came time for visiting teams to play at the Spectrum in Philadelphia, some opposing players would suddenly come down with something; they'd say they were sick. Perhaps they were, at the thought of facing the Bullies. The syndrome became known round the NHL, but its origins go back to Flin Flon. The "Flin Flon flu." In Clarke's day it was quite contagious in Manitoba.

"Our coach, Brian Shaw, used to tell us that there are lots of miners out there [in the Flin Flon stands]. He would say, 'Make sure you stay three feet from the boards. If you get close enough, they will take a poke at you,'" Perreault says with a laugh. "I don't know how many teams won up there. We were about the only team that ever won up in Flin Flon."

When Perreault arrived in Flin Flon, he knew what was coming. It likely didn't help his cause that Moose Jaw listed Perreault as 6'1" and 205 pounds. Two hundred and five pounds was a big boy in the late 1960s. Maybe Moose Jaw wanted to sell a few more seats, but Perreault did not weigh that much. "I got a laugh at that. I was six one. I was in awesome shape. I used to do isometrics. I ran every day. I skipped rope every day. I was in really good shape. I was 167 pounds both years of Junior," he chuckles.

Perhaps Perreault's listed size made him a target, or maybe word had been going around the league that the kid was good to go. Whatever it was, his first trip to Flin Flon was a memorable one. For the record, he did not come down with the flu. "I think I had five fights my first game in Flin Flon. I got in a fight with a guy named Jack Criel. He was really strong. I hit him with a couple punches and he didn't go down. He just kept going and I always respected him for that. We shook hands after the game. You get respect even from players that you play against. You hate them when you're on the ice, but once you're off the ice, you're just another player."

Perreault survived Flin Flon, but he still had to survive the rest of the league. Another night in Junior he was facing off against the Estevan Bruins. Future NHLer Jim Harrison was a mainstay on the team. He would go on to a life in the pros in the NHL and WHA. In fact, a few years before Darryl Sittler set an NHL record for most points in a single game with 10 against the Boston Bruins, Harrison did the same thing in the WHA. In January 1973 he had 3 goals and 7 assists for 10 points in an Alberta Oilers WHA win over the New York Raiders. When Harrison first crossed paths with Perreault, he was Estevan's second-highest scorer, and penalty minutes leader. "Our captain, Reg Bechtold, said, 'You really got to watch Jim Harrison. He'll try to catch you off guard if you get in a fight with him.'"

Perreault and the Moose Jaw Canucks hit the ice against the Estevan Bruins. Soon enough the gloves hit the ice. Perreault was in a fight. But he wasn't having a go with Harrison. He was trading punches with one of Harrison's teammates. And Perreault, as hockey players like to say, was doing well. He cut up his opponent. Leaving his bloody Estevan counterpart behind, Perreault made his way past Harrison. He took one look at the Estevan scorer and tough guy and issued a stern warning: *You're next!* "Honestly, I think he thought I was nuts. But I never had to deal with him for the two years that I played in Junior."

Sometimes the best fights are the ones you don't have to have. Perreault was gaining a rep as a tough player, one who could take care of business with his fists if it was called for, but perhaps equally—if not more—important, with a steady body check. Aside from Clarke and Leach, the western league that Perreault skated in featured a few other players who would go on to win two Stanley Cups in a row with the Philadelphia Flyers. Orest Kindrachuk, never one to shy away from a fight or a scuffle, played for the Saskatoon Blades. Before he became known around the hockey world as "The Hammer," future *Sports Illustrated* cover boy Dave Schultz skated for the Swift Current Broncos. And the "Big Bird," Don Saleski, was a right-winger for the Regina Pats. "Brian Shaw used to have me do what today would be considered stupid things," says Perreault. "We hated Regina. Don Saleski played for them. Don was a big guy. I think the hardest hit I have ever given was a hit on Saleski at centre ice. I knocked him out cold. It scared me because he tried to get up and he fell on his face again."

When his Junior career ended, the pros came calling for Richie Perreault. He was invited to Chicago Blackhawks training camp. Aside from being a top-notch hockey player, he was also a star on the baseball field. (He still is. In 2019, Perreault's slow-pitch team won gold at the Alberta 55 Plus Summer Games.) More than fifty years ago, just a week before he was set to head to Blackhawks training camp, Richie was playing baseball. "I ended up running into my second baseman and I broke my collarbone."

This was in the unforgiving era of old-school hockey. Perreault of course could not go to camp and the Blackhawks weren't going to sit around and wait for him to get healthy. Billy Reay was the head coach of the Blackhawks. He let Richie know what he thought of his decision to play baseball a week before an NHL camp: "He ended up telling me, 'You don't think much of your hockey career, if you're playing baseball for a bush-league team like St. Albert.' To me that just turned me right off the pros."

And that was that. If that's how the pros were going to treat a guy, Perreault really didn't want to have anything to do with them. Once his collarbone healed, he found a team to play for: the St. Albert Comets of the Edmonton Central Hockey League. It was nothing fancy, but it was good hockey, and it was home. "There were lots of real good hockey players in that league. There were lots of guys who could have turned pro. A lot of them had the talent but they didn't, like a Mark Messier, have that mean streak. With a guy like Messier, you'd always be looking over your shoulder saying, 'Where is Messier?'"

Perreault picked up a job working in construction and then got a job with the city of St. Albert. He'd work during the day and then play games at night. The drives to games around the Edmonton area weren't too long. The Comets would play around Edmonton in places like Fort Saskatchewan, Sherwood Park, and Leduc. Perreault stood out right away. "He could stick-handle. He was a great skater. He was big, strong. He could really shoot the puck, and he was just an intimidating guy. He was so big and strong," says his old Comets goaltender Zane Jakubec, a retired St. Albert phys ed teacher.

"He was pretty quiet. I used to dress next to him for two or three years. He didn't do a lot of talking. He came and put his stuff on, and he went out and performed. He was just an awesome hockey player. He was playing probably at 210 to 215 pounds, with a body fat of five or six percent. He was a specimen. A great skater. He saw the ice. He was tougher than nails. And he could shoot rockets. He had it all," says Jakubec.

Jakubec makes a point of reminding me that the ECHL was no scrub league. "We ended up with a lot of guys on the Comets that had played for the [University of Alberta] Golden Bears and we also had ex-Junior players. It wasn't beer-league hockey. We practiced once or twice a week and we played two times a week. It was a commitment.

"The little towns that supported Senior hockey in the seventies, they really came out. On a good night we would have five hundred to seven hundred people in the stands. For a city of ten thousand, that's not bad."

That's when Perreault caught the eye of future NHLer Troy Murray. Who wouldn't love a player who could score, hit, and fight? By all accounts, Richie was a nice guy; in fact, he was even nice enough to drive an opponent to a game. Guys in the area didn't always play for their hometown teams. One night a buddy of Richie's, named Wayne Rimmer, who was playing against him and the Comets that night, asked Richie if he could get a ride to the game with him. No problem. Once they got to the arena, Richie went to the Comets' room and Wayne went the other way. Soon enough, the carpool buddies ran into each other on the ice. Rimmer was a big man: 6'3" and 220 pounds. He took up a lot of room in the front seat on the way to the game and he took up a lot of room on the ice, too. With Wayne running around too much for Richie's liking, the pair soon dropped the gloves: "He was running at one of my other players. I always took care of the other players on my team," says Perreault.

"My mom and dad were at the game. I was a little late getting out of the dressing room afterward. Wayne went up to my mom and dad and said, 'Mr. and Mrs. Perreault, do you think Rich is going to give me a ride home?' My dad told him, 'Once you guys step off the ice you guys are friends again.' I always laugh at that. We had a good laugh on the ride back.

"I know Wayne even today. It's funny when you talk about that stuff years later. It was good. He respected me and the way I took care of my teammates."

One of the highlights for Perreault during his years with the Comets was a chance, one night at their tiny little rink in St. Albert, to play a game against the Polish national team. That may sound strange, but in winter 1974 the Polish national hockey team, who had finished fifth in the previous spring's Ice Hockey World Championship, were on a Canadian tour. On the night of January 4, 1974, they showed up at the St. Albert Arena.

As Ray Turchansky wrote the next day in the *Edmonton Journal*: "Fans weren't hanging from the rafters, but they were sitting on them." Eight hundred and fifty fans swarmed into the tiny rink that could usually only hold six hundred and fifty or so. The rink only had seats on one side of the building, and they were packed, with the rest of the fans surrounding the ice on the other side of the barn. Bodies were everywhere, as further evidenced by the *Journal*'s account of the night: "A freelance photographer had his foot go through the concession area ceiling while attempting to balance along roofing beams while reaching his catwalk seat."

As for Team Poland, "We knew nothing about them," says Jakubec, who split the goaltending duties that night.

It turns out the players from Poland were pretty good. They were up 2–0 in the second when Perreault scored for the Comets to make it a 2–1 game. The night ended in a 9–3 Poland win. That night is one of the reasons Perreault played in his hometown. The rink was packed, and his number one supporter was in the stands. "His mom was his biggest fan. She was out there every game," says Jakubec.

These days you don't see a lot of postgame write-ups like that one. In the same article that mentioned the photographer's foot, this is how the Perreault goal is described: "Richie Perreault flipped in the rebound from 15 feet. 'Guess whose boy that is?' shouted Perreault's mother, perched above the goal judge's catwalk."

"Oh my goodness," laughs Richie. "My mom was probably our loudest fan; she'd be in one corner and my dad would be in the far corner away from her. She was awesome. She never missed a game."

Just like her son, she'd get in the odd tilt at a game, or at least the threat of one: "One time it was in the Westlock arena—all of a sudden there was a fight. There was a woman fighting in the stands."

Perreault looked up into the stands and saw the fists flying. Were his worst fears about to come true? Was his mother, the nice lady who drove him all around St. Albert during his minor hockey days—was she throwing down in the stands? Luckily, no. Richie could breathe easy. "I looked up and it wasn't my mom. It was one of the guys' wives. She ended up getting in a scrap. I thought, 'Oh my goodness. I'm glad it wasn't my mom.'"

Richie enjoyed life with the Comets. He loved playing in front of his mother, his father, and the rest of his family. He enjoyed the camaraderie of the game. The pros liked him enough to come calling again. Legendary NHL goaltender Tiny Thompson, a four-time Vezina Trophy winner and a Hockey Hall of Famer, was now in the scouting business, with the Bruins. He and another scout asked Perreault about turning pro. He politely declined.

After a few years the Comets folded. Perreault went to play in Stony Plain. The Stony Plain Eagles had a Hall of Fame connection, too. Their head coach was Chicago Blackhawks legend Glen Hall. "He told me, 'Would you like to have a tryout with the Oilers?'"

That would be the Edmonton Oilers of the WHA. Perreault had some friends playing with them. Guys like Edgar "Rusty" Patenaude, Barry Long, and Ray McKay, whom he had played Junior with in Moose Jaw. Once again, he passed on the chance to turn pro: "I don't know why. I said, 'Thank you, but no thank you.'"

In fact, he had many reasons for staying where he was. Family was one, as were the bonds he was forming on the ice and in the room with his teammates. What Billy Reay said to him all those years ago lingered in his mind. He also spoke to former teammates who had left St. Albert, who had left Alberta to try their luck at the professional game. "You played around here because you had family around here. I remember talking to kids from the west who went to play pro in the east. Those guys didn't associate much with westerners. If you were an eastern player, you'd get more ice time. I thought, 'That's funny. You know, why would you do that?' I was never part of that culture. When you're a team you are family."

After just seven games with Stony Plain, Richie joined a different Oilers team, the Hobbema Oilers. At the time Hobbema was called a "Native" team. They played Senior hockey and in Native tournaments throughout the west and beyond. It was an eye-opening experience for Perreault, an Indigenous man who grew up in St. Albert. "Every weekend we would play five games. They hired me as a player-coach."

The hockey was good. It was life off the ice that was a little different, and eye-opening, for Richie. "They only spoke Cree in the dressing room. The players used to tell jokes and laugh, and I didn't understand what they were saying. I didn't speak Cree. My mom and dad spoke Cree, but they never taught us. Somehow the guys found out that I did not understand Cree. Dennis Buffalo was our captain. One day the guys started to speak English. I pulled Dennis aside."

Richie wanted to know what was happening. Why were the guys no longer speaking their first language? Why was a team that only spoke Cree now suddenly speaking English? "He said, 'Rich, we all respect you and we realize you don't understand Cree, and we don't want you thinking that we're talking about you.' I said, 'No, no. The dressing room should be Cree; that's important.' 'No,' he said, 'it was a unanimous decision, we are going to speak English.' I told him, 'I wish you wouldn't, because we have a great team here and we have a great team spirit.'"

The Hobbema Oilers were really good. Richie tells me that at least three of the guys on the team could have turned pro, but just like him, they were happy playing at home. The experience gave Richie a chance, he says, to play with "my people." It was also a learning experience in many ways.

"We always shook hands at the end of games. The first time I shook hands after the game, the guys on the other team had really limp handshakes." The limp handshakes were accompanied by the players not even looking Richie in the eye. He grew up in the world of firm postgame handshakes and eye contact. He turned to one of his teammates and asked what was going on. "He said, 'That's a sign of respect.'"

Growing up in St. Albert, Richie was removed from Cree culture. Now he was becoming a part of it. "It was great. You don't realize what they themselves have to go through. I was always there to learn from them."

The Hobbema Oilers didn't only play in an Alberta Senior league and in Native tournaments in the west. Perreault and the Oilers traveled to Europe and the United States for tournaments: "We'd go to Germany and France. We had a really good team. The first time we played on the bigger international ice we played Finland. They had quite a few ex–Maple Leafs on their team."

The Oilers were introduced to a new style of play. The Finns would hold on to the puck as much as they could. They did not play the Canadian dump-and-chase style: "They would go in on a three-on-two and then they'd throw it back, turn around, and go again. They beat us eight to two."

There was only one thing the Oilers could do if they wanted to compete at this tournament: change. The player-coach had a plan. After the game Richie laid down the new game plan for his

Oilers: "'What we have to do—and we're not used to doing this—is let them handle the puck along the boards and we will cut the ice down to our side.' We did so, and it worked. We ended up meeting Finland in the final. The winning team got gold watches. We ended up beating them two to one."

Perreault never fully stopped playing hockey. And he only just recently retired. And I mean recently. He played hockey in the winter, baseball in the summer, and kept working for the city of St. Albert well into his mid-seventies.

The glory days of the Comets and of Senior hockey in town became memories, but memories that never went away. "When I worked for the city of St. Albert, we were shoveling a pathway to get from one street to another. This gentleman at the time, it was probably a dozen years ago, he goes past me, and he turns around and he says, 'You wouldn't happen to be Richard Perreault?' I said, 'Yep.' 'Oh my God,' he says. 'We always used to enjoy those Comet games.' I said, 'We had the best fans in the world. It's nice to meet you.'"

St. Albert has become a name that hockey fans know. Perry Pearn's Hockey Camps are legendary in Edmonton hockey circles. NHLers and other pros hit the ice in August every year to get in shape for the upcoming season at the camp. Perry Pearn didn't run the camp alone; he did it with the help of Perreault's old teammate Zane Jakubec, who can easily rhyme off some of the players who have skated at the St. Albert camp over the years: "Johnny Boychuk, Daymond Langkow. Right now, from the league, Jordan Martinook, Sammy Steele."

If you don't know St. Albert from the Pearn camp, turn over some of the hockey cards in your collection. Mark Messier, Jarome Iginla, Jamie McLennan, Colton Parayko, Tyson Jost, Nick

Holden, and the kid who used to watch the Comets, Troy Murray, all hail from Perrault's hometown. Messier and Murray had arenas in St. Albert named after them. The town is bigger now; there's more than just the one rink. A few years ago, when Murray was back in his hometown, he mentioned Perreault in a speech he was giving about his minor hockey days and growing up in the city. "That meant a lot," says the old hockey player.

All those years ago, when Richie was playing for Moose Jaw and Calgary in Junior, he'd hear the name-calling. He'd hear the racist taunts. Some of it was from the players, but most of it was from the stands. His old buddy Zane knows what he had to go through just to play the game he loves: "He had to fight discrimination and racism." Zane doesn't even want to utter the words that would come down from the stands.

All those years ago, Richie decided to ignore the racists in the stands and the taunts on the ice. He just kept playing. Hockey became his equalizer: "I just turned my head and I thought, 'Don't even go there. You're only going to make it worse.' I had to forget it."

He has been playing hockey his entire life and he's still in great shape. "I always run into my neighbour, Brandon, because I'm always picking up leaves and everything. He says, 'Richie, you could still play.' I laugh. I'm seventy-five years old."

In those seventy-five years, even though Richie didn't go pro, he still became a St. Albert legend and he got to connect with those he coined "my people" when he played with Hobbema. The taunts became plaudits. He played the game because he loved it. What has hockey given Richie Perreault? "Everything. You got a lot of respect. And honestly, you made friends with the guys that you played against. It's special, it's a family you grew up playing with and against. It's like a family even with the guys you played against.

"I ended up playing in a fifty-and-over league in St. Albert. I was on the same team with a couple of brothers, good hockey players. They told me they used to play against me. They said, 'When we used to play against you, when you played for Hobbema, everybody hated you. But I know—now—that you got my back.'

"I said, 'That's the way I grew up.' And they said, 'We always respected you. But we hated you at the same time.'"

"Richie was the man," repeats Murray. "I think he was happy with his life and what he had and playing for the Comets was good enough for him."

Richie Perreault, wearing the captain's C, second from the right, front row, with the legendary St. Albert Comets.

CHAPTER 14

Ken "Cowboy" McTeer

Kimberley, British Columbia

"**E**verybody knew everybody," begins Terry Leal, who grew up in Kimberley, British Columbia, before he left town for university in 1963. "The town was really close-knit. The guys worked with each other, and everybody had a nickname. They called my dad Big Aub—he was a big guy. Six foot two and 220 pounds. And my name was Cheeks because I ripped the ass out of my ski pants up on the ski hill."

Everyone in the mining town of Kimberley has a handle. When Ken McTeer moved from Calgary, Alberta, hardly anyone called him Ken. "Most of the time we called him Cowboy," says Cheeks. Ken "Cowboy" McTeer was one of the hundreds of men in town who worked for Cominco, the company that owned the town's mines, which tore into the beautiful southwestern British Columbia hills in search of lead, zinc, and silver. Cowboy didn't simply move to Kimberley for the job; he had a pretty good side gig as well as the top centre for the Kimberley Dynamiters of the Western International Hockey League (WIHL). Cheeks grew up just a few blocks away from Cowboy and his then wife, Jean: "I liked the McTeers from the get-go. Ken's wife was my teacher in grade five. She is still alive and lives in Kimberley. She was my favourite teacher of all time."

Cowboy was one of Cheeks's all-time favourite players: "He was an outstanding hockey player. Probably one of the best that ever played for the Dynamiters."

Cowboy's hockey life started in Calgary. He was born and bred in the Stampede City when the population was only about 150,000. Ken played for the Calgary Buffaloes of the Western Canada Junior Hockey League for a couple of seasons. At the time, the league was made up of seven teams. Ken would spend his winters on the bus and on the ice traveling the circuit to Edmonton, Regina, Moose Jaw, Medicine Hat, and a few other places. His play was good enough to get himself more than a sniff from the Chicago Blackhawks. He attended two Chicago training camps, but he never caught on with the big club in the Original Six era. So instead of heading south, Ken ended up doing what thousands of young Canadian men have done over the years—he headed west.

Packing up and leaving Calgary was an easy decision. Cowboy was in his early twenties, but his ties to the city were already mostly severed. He had lost his father, Archibald, a few years earlier. Archibald McTeer, who was a decent hockey player himself, contracted a disease while fighting for Canada in Europe during World War II. He died shortly after returning home to Calgary. Cowboy wasn't tight with his uncles, so he hit the road. His first stop, in the fall of 1954, wasn't Kimberley. It was Trail, British Columbia, home of the legendary Smoke Eaters of the WIHL.

The Smoke Eaters came by their name honestly. If you lived in Trail, smoke—and basically eating it—was a fact of life. It was the home of the Trail Smelter. It had been a fixture in the town since 1895, processing lead and zinc ore coming up from the nearby mines. The smokestacks of the smelter produced clouds of sulphur dioxide that filled the air of Trail and fell into the forests and farmlands around town. Aside from the jobs it produced, the smelter was also an excellent recruiting tool for hockey players. The team could say, "Come play hockey for us and we will give you a job at the smelter." That's exactly what the Smoke Eaters did with Calgary's Ken McTeer. He arrived in town and scored twenty goals for the Smoke Eaters that season, while spending the rest of his time at his day job at the smelter.

Even with that draw, there was not enough work in Trail to keep McTeer around; he lasted just one year with the Smoke Eaters. McTeer was released by the team just a few years before it would go on to win the World Hockey Championship. He wasn't out of work or off the ice for long; there was another mining town, Kimberley, just three hours east of Trail, also run by Cominco. Their team, the Kimberley Dynamiters, was one of the archrivals of the Smoke Eaters. "At that time, Cominco pretty much ran Kimberley," says Cowboy's youngest son, Pat McTeer. "They were operating the lead and zinc mines and they gave everybody really good jobs. It was always a decent option to come to this area."

So, in fall 1955, Ken McTeer took up residence in Kimberley, and it didn't take long for "Ken" to become "Cowboy." People found out he was from Calgary, and though likely not the most original name, it stuck. Cowboy got a job with Cominco at the Sullivan Mine's surveying department, which meant he only had to go underground on occasion. And like most stories go, he met a girl—Jean—who would become his wife. They raised their two sons in Kimberley before parting ways years later. Terry was born in 1958. Pat came a couple of years later. In between working at the mine and being a husband and a dad, Cowboy also became a local hockey legend.

Over the phone, my new friend, Terry "Cheeks" Leal, tells me there was only one place to be on a cold winter's night in Kimberley: "I remember going to Dynamiters games when my dad had his '41 Plymouth. Of course, the rink wasn't heated, and it was cold as hell. The weather back then always seemed to be a lot colder and there was a lot more snow than what this area gets now."

Cheeks's dad, Big Aub, was an executive of the Dynamiters for twenty-five years. He and the rest of the execs would not sit in their reserved seats; instead they'd pace above the stands, stressing over every play taking place on the ice. At the same time, young Cheeks, maybe ten or eleven years old, would be keeping an eye on his grade-five teacher's husband, Cowboy McTeer, centering the Dynamiter's top line, against opponents like the Smoke Eaters, the Nelson Maple Leafs, or the Spokane Flyers. "Kenny was a smooth skater," says Cheeks. "He'd go in the corners and fish the puck out or he'd bring it out himself. A lot of times he would start the rush. He was a goal scorer, too."

McTeer and his linemates, a couple of guys named Les Lilley and Walt Peacosh, made up the team's top line, dubbed the "Nitro Line." (Get it?) It was the perfect name for a line that would light up the WIHL. Lilley was a tall local boy from Kimberley. Peacosh had made his way to town all the way from The Pas, Manitoba. "The Nitro Line was the number one line for the Dynamiters. They would sometimes finish one through three in scoring in the WIHL. The Dynamiters to me, growing up, were everything. I idolized them," says Cheeks.

The Dynamiters were the talk of Kimberley. Sure, everyone had a favourite NHL team—Cheeks liked the Maple Leafs—but their games were beamed into town from a faraway land. The miners would jam into the local rink, and the kids would talk about what the Dynamiters did over the weekend before and after school on Mondays. Kimberley was growing; so much so, in fact, that the town built a new rink in 1961. The Kimberley Civic Centre is one of those classic old rinks with the rolling, barn-type roof. It seats around 2,400 fans, and the Kootenay Rockies provide the perfect backdrop. The McTeer boys were growing up, too. A couple of years after the Civic Centre arrived, Terry started to form his first memories of his dad on the ice with the Dynamiters. He watched them from as up close as he could: "Front row. We had season tickets and my maternal grandfather took me to all those games. From a very young age I was watching Dad play."

It didn't take young Terry very long to realize that his dad, Ken, was a pretty good hockey player. He wasn't out there playing pickup games like some of the other dads in town: he had rare gifts. "My grandfather would obviously point things out. Dad never talked about it [his hockey career] that much himself. The only time you ever saw him get excited about sport were the times he was playing golf—and that was usually because he was mad," says Terry. "When it came to hockey, even as a kid, I could tell Dad was a unique talent, watching his line scoring the goals. He was centre ice on the Nitro Line. I can't remember if he ever won the scoring title in the league, but they only played forty games or so every year, and how do you get a hundred points in forty games? That takes a special talent."

Terry and his brother Pat were "Cowboy's sons." And Cowboy

was the man around town: "Dad was well-known. They were *the* sports team in town. Dad was a very popular player along with his linemates."

The Dynamiters were local kings. After the game the beer would flow, often freely, at a local bar or two around town. "Kimberley wasn't a big town then; it still isn't," Terry tells me. "I'm not sure how to describe it, but when he went uptown, everyone knew who Cowboy was."

But when Monday morning rolled around, it was back to work at the Sullivan Mine, Ken sometimes sporting the odd hockey battle scar or two from the weekend. "He came home from one road trip—I think they were in Nelson or Trail—on the Saturday or Sunday night, and he had two black eyes and stitches over both of his eyebrows. My brother and I were horrified," says Terry. "I don't know if he got hit in the face with the puck, got high-sticked, or got into a fight. He never would say."

Cowboy led the Dynamiters to the WIHL championship, the Savage Cup, in the spring of 1964. That Savage Cup win put the Dynamiters up against the Lacombe Rockets in the Allan Cup quarterfinals. The Dynamiters dropped the first two games in the best-of-five series in Lacombe, Alberta, then they headed back home and won game three. Cowboy had a four-point night in game four—his goal and three assists, along with a hat trick by his Nitro Line winger, Walt Peacosh, led the Dynamiters to an 8–5 win. The series was tied 2–2, with the fifth and final game set for the next night in Kimberley.

The headline of the April 3, 1964, edition of the *Red Deer Advocate* summed up game five perfectly: "Allan Cup Bid of Rockets Snuffed Out by 'Nitro Line.'" Just over two thousand of Kimberley's finest—miners, teachers, schoolkids, and whoever else could fit into the Civic Centre—watched the Dynamiters skate to a 7–4 win to earn a spot in the Allan Cup semifinal. Cowboy scored two of the Nitro Line's five goals that night. Lilley had two and Peacosh scored one. In typical Cowboy fashion, Cowboy added two assists for a four-point night in the decisive game.

The Dynamiters went on to get swept by Saskatoon in the Allan Cup semis, but Ken McTeer's place as a Kimberley and WIHL star was cemented. The next year the Nelson Maple Leafs won the Savage Cup. Back in those days, winning teams could pick up a star or two from around their league to help with their Allan Cup run. (In that era of the six NHL teams, the Allan Cup was the second-best trophy in hockey.) The Maple Leafs chose the now thirty-year-old Cowboy and Peacosh. In the national semifinals, Nelson lined up against the challengers all the way from Warroad, Minnesota. Cowboy scored a goal in the Maple Leafs series, clinching a 6–3 game four win. Cowboy and the rest of his new teammates hopped on a plane and headed for Sherbrooke, Quebec. That entire best-of-seven series would be played in Sherbrooke.

The Sherbrooke Beavers set the tone for the series when they scored just ten seconds into what would be their 7–3 game one win. After the Maple Leafs dropped game two 4–1, Nelson player-coach Bobby Kromm voiced his displeasure with referee William "Dutch" Van Deelen of Edmonton. He went to the media, demanding the referee be removed from the series. Perhaps Kromm's complaints had something to do with his on-ice stick-jousting with Sherbrooke player-coach George Roy. Kromm even took a swing at one Sherbrooke fan during the game. The rest of the series was more of the same—the Beavers won game three 9–2 and game four 8–4 to sweep the series and win the

Canadian title. As for Van Deelen, he was still around for game four. Kromm was also around for most of it, at least until the third period, when he was kicked out of the game for trying to club Van Deelen with his stick. McTeer didn't score a goal in the series. It was the closest he ever came to an Allan Cup.

As his sons say, Cowboy didn't talk too much about his hockey career. However, in late December 1966, McTeer was part of a game that everyone around the WIHL was talking about. Cowboy and the league's best players were selected to play on an all-star team to face off in Trail against the touring Soviet Red Army Selects—yes, the WIHL had a summit series long before the famous 1972 series. "It was incredible," says Terry McTeer. "I had heard of the Red Army at that point, and we knew who the Russians were, always winning the Olympic Games and the World Championships. I remember very little of it because it was over fifty years ago, but it was fast."

The Cominco Arena in Trail held four thousand fans and it was packed that night. Les Lilley, Cowboy's old winger on the Nitro Line, was the head coach of the WIHL All-Stars. He took Cowboy and five other players from the Dynamiters to play in the game. No one was surprised when the Nitro Line, now made up of Cowboy, Dick Vincent, and Walt Peacosh, connected for a goal: Peacosh lit the lamp in a 5–4 win for the All-Stars over the Red Army Selects. It was the first of nine games for the Russians on that December 1966 cross-Canada tour. "They beat the Russians and the place went crazy"—that's the memory that lingers in the mind of Terry McTeer.

A few months later, on March 3, 1967, the Kimberley Dynamiters held a "Kenny 'Cowboy' McTeer Nite" (*sic*). Cowboy was packing it in, retiring. But the Dynamiters were not just going to let him glide off the ice. They would say goodbye in style.

That night is the first hockey memory Pat McTeer has of his dad. Pat's older brother, Terry, was nine years old and used to the limelight; Pat was just starting to realize what a big deal around town his old man was. "It was the night before I turned five. I had never seen him play. I have no recollection of him playing because I was too young, but that was a pretty overwhelming night at the Kimberly Civic Centre.

"They were playing the Rossland Warriors that night. They had a huge ceremony before the game. There were dignitaries from the city. They presented him with all kinds of gifts. My grandmother, his mother—they brought her out from Calgary. My brother got a full set of hockey gear—he was four years older than me, so he was probably ready to play hockey. I got a bicycle. Even the Snow Fiesta queen was out there. They used to have a little beauty pageant in the wintertime. Of course, my mom was out on the ice as well."

Mom got a gift from the Dynamiters, too, although Pat can't remember what it was. As for Dad, he got the perfect retirement gift: a recliner chair.

Cowboy was done, at least for the time being. He made a comeback with the Dynamiters a couple of years later, but then settled into life with an old-timers team. It was basically the same bunch of guys he played with in his Dynamiter days, and not surprisingly, they went on to win a couple of Canadian old-timers championships. Pat eventually grew out of his bike; young Terry grew out of his hockey gear; and Cowboy's old recliner went where most old recliners go after a few years, away. But there was one thing from "Cowboy Nite" that stuck around the McTeer house for years: "A great big piece of plywood," says Pat. "It was all painted up with a little donkey—and Dad was standing on top of it, with skates on and a cowboy hat. He was painted really big, with a big head. It was quite funny. We incorporated it into our rumpus room."

The rumpus room was the venue of many an indoor hockey game between the brothers. If a stick got up too high and perhaps put a dent in the ceiling tile, Cowboy would have to lay down the law. That did not go over well with the boys, but they knew how to take out their aggression: "My brother and I, when we would be in trouble, we would throw darts at the painting." That old piece of plywood would eventually disappear, too. "I wish I still had it, to be honest," says Pat.

Cowboy eventually retired from the mine. He took a job with the city of Kimberley as an economic development officer before becoming a sales rep for Kootenay Beer. His sons, teenagers by this point, did not mind this. "We used to drive Mom crazy," says Terry. "We had an indoor garage in the house, but you couldn't use it because there was usually a pallet of beer cases in there.

"People would come by the house and they'd say, 'Cowboy said we could have ten cases for the wedding.' So, we'd go in the garage and get them the cases."

Cowboy and his wife, Jean, eventually split up, but Cowboy never left Kimberley. He may have been from Calgary, but this tiny little town in the East Kootenays became his home. "You get a job, you start to work, you're playing hockey. . . . I think it gave him a sense of purpose," Terry tells me.

"I've seen this over the years myself—it was just a great bunch of guys who really connected well," Pat says of teammates whom Cowboy met and grew old with in Kimberley. "They did everything together, even outside of hockey. They all played ball, they all played golf, they all drank beer. I really think that was it. Kimberley is just a beautiful place to be. It's peace and quiet. It's got everything outdoorsy that you would ever want to do. It is a four-season place. You're not terribly far away from the big city if you want to be there. I think that's the huge charm of Kimberley and it keeps people here. I know a lot of people who say they want to leave; but it's amazing how many people come back here."

Once McTeer got to Kimberley he never left. He was a fit for the town and the town was a fit for him. He passed away, in Kimberley, on October 26, 2018. Terry Leal, who as a kid idolized McTeer, had become a lifelong friend. "He was a fantastic hockey player, but he was also a fantastic individual. We visited him when he was on his final legs. He was at a special care home in Kimberley. I can always remember, my wife and me, we'd go to visit him. By then he couldn't speak. But all you had to do was look at his eyes. He would get emotional. He was so caring with the way he looked back at you and when you left, he would cry."

The WIHL folded in the 1980s. The Sullivan Mine is also closed now, and Cominco is long gone. You can visit the Sullivan Mine Interpretive Centre in Kimberley if you want to see what life was like for Cowboy and the thousands of others who worked in the mines. Terry Leal moved to Cranbrook and is now a retired accountant. Cowboy's oldest son, Terry, is retired and lives in Victoria. As for Pat, he still lives in Kimberley. The area is now a golfer's paradise. Pat is the superintendent at Bootleg Gap Golf Course, where Cowboy's celebration of life was held after he passed away. Kimberly had one final chance to say goodbye to one of their old Dynamiters: "I always thought all these guys were born fifteen years too early. Most of them would have been NHL players, no question, if there'd been more than six teams," says

Pat. "Look at the Trail Smoke Eaters. They won the World Championship in 1961. Outside the NHL, they were the best hockey team in the world. That's the way it was back then," says Pat.

I ask Pat my last questions: Did that bother his dad? Was he upset that he had to work at a mine and play in Kimberley instead of the NHL?

A short pause on the line. But then the answer comes through clear as a bell.

"No."

Ken "Cowboy" McTeer, in the middle, centering the famed Nitro Line with Les Lilley (left) and Walt Peacosh (right).

Wayne Woodacre

Pictou, Nova Scotia

It's incredible the impact a local hockey star can have on a small town and on the young people who live there. That player, just doing what he loves to do by simply playing every Saturday night, can fuel the passion of a young fan and make an impact that lasts a lifetime. Take my old hockey hero, the guy everyone called "T-Pot," for instance. He had no idea of the impression he was making on the young kids of Pictou, Nova Scotia—very much including me—by just playing. On the phone, he tells me, "To be honest, I had no idea whatsoever. I just loved to play."

T-Pot eventually caught on. The entire town seemed to love T-Pot and the Mariners. When you have a town of 5,000 folks and you jam 1,500 of them into a rink, it does seem like the entire town is behind you. Eventually that became obvious to T. Goal after goal, championship after championship, the love kept adding up: "You'd be walking down the street, cars would drive by you, and kids would be hollering, 'T-Pot! T-Pot!' Everywhere you went people were hollering my name. People were watching you do whatever you were doing."

By the mid-1980s, T-Pot was just the latest local legend to

skate in my town. Before him there were scoring legends like Tic William, Mark Babineau, and Kenny Paquet. After him came Joey MacDonald, who skated at Hector Arena and ended up as a goalie in the NHL. Just before T-Pot played for the Mariners, though, there was another hockey legend who tore up the local Junior and Town League scene, scoring goals by the hundreds. Before I was a ten-year-old rink rat at Hector Arena, T-Pot was a ten-year-old rink rat at the same arena, and he had a local hockey hero as well: Wayne Woodacre. "I was just a kid, probably less than ten, watching Wayne play hockey. I went to all the Junior games. I was a rink rat sitting up in the rafters, watching the boys play. He was a young man, too, probably only five or six years older than me. I idolized him."

Woodacre was the star player for the Pictou Junior B Maripacs in the late 1970s, having come up through Pictou's minor hockey system during the decade. There were no big-rep teams to play for back then. You played for your hometown, and Wayne repre-sented Pictou better than anyone. He led both his Peewee league and Bantam teams in scoring. In Bantam he was a Provincial Tournament All-Star. In 1975–76 he was the MVP at the Nova Scotia Midget Provincial Tournament. Then he moved on to Ju-nior B hockey, where he starred for the Maripacs, the predecessor to T-Pot's Pictou Mariners teams a few years later. A few years before my buddies and I were dying to wear T-Pot's number 8, T-Pot was dying to wear Woodacre's own number 8: "I wore eight because of him. I idolized the hell out of Woodacre and watched all [his] Junior games," says T-Pot. "As soon as I had a chance to get on a team, I wore his number. It was my sweater, and I didn't let go of it."

It was a time in the game when the local stars of most Nova Scotia towns didn't stray very far from home. One season Wayne finished tied for the league scoring lead with Mike McPhee, a player from the Port Hawkesbury Strait Pirates. McPhee left the following season to play NCAA hockey for Rensselaer Polytechnic Institute in Troy, New York, and went on to win the Stanley Cup with the Montreal Canadiens in 1986. Wayne kept playing Junior B. He stayed in his hometown.

In the late 1970s, Junior B hockey was king in Pictou County, and Wayne became a scoring star known throughout the league. Wayne's Maripacs defeated the Stellarton Stewart's Jackets 6–3 in game seven of the 1979 Northumberland Junior B League semifinals in front of 2,266 fans at Pictou's Hector Arena. It was the largest crowd to attend a game in Pictou in six years. Wayne didn't disappoint, scoring the opener sixty-one seconds into the game and adding another in the 6–3 win, in what Stephen Goodwin, a local sports reporter for the *Evening News*, called Wayne's "superb series" in the smoke-filled venue. (Goodwin even pleaded with the public in his column, "If anything can be asked for the next series between Antigonish and Pictou, it is that the smokers stop smoking when they enter the rinks. With the arenas jammed and half the fans billowing smoke, the players are working many times as hard and inhale that much more smoke.")

Apparently, there was not enough smoke to deter the Antigonish Bulldogs in that series against Pictou. Antigonish ended up winning the Northumberland and the Nova Scotia Junior B titles. And Wayne kept playing for the Maripacs year after year. In 1981, his final year of Junior, he led the Maripacs in scoring, finished second in the league, and was named Pictou's MVP. "As a

Junior he was dynamite," says T-Pot. "And we said it for years—he could have played in the NHL."

But, like so many hometown heroes, life had other plans: Wayne met a girl named Ruth and was married at the age of twenty. When I ask Ruth to recall the glory days of her husband's career, she responds, "Oh gosh, there are some things I probably shouldn't remember and then there are some things I probably shouldn't be telling you. I was chasing after Woody and dating him. When I got mixed up with him, I can remember the excitement of the hockey. He'd pick me up and we'd go to the games. We'd go up to Stellarton for a game. In the playoffs it would be crazy there. I came from the country. I wasn't always going to hockey games, so this was pretty exciting for me. Our fans would all be on one side and Wayne would be on the ice with the rest of the team. Wayne's team would usually be winning and then there would be fighting. And the next thing you know there were glass pint bottles coming across the whole surface of the ice and breaking on the beams above our heads. Good times. I thought, 'I like this. This is going to be fun. This is going to be fun!' I was just a kid."

Ruth kept going to the games and Wayne kept scoring. He had the best wrist shot a player could ask for. I say this because I know: Wayne was my coach during my first year of Bantam hockey. He'd rip a wrister during practice and leave a bunch of teenage boys speechless. "His wrist shot was the best," says Ruth. "That was his bread and butter. He loved that wrist shot."

When Wayne's Junior career ended, he stayed in Pictou. He worked at the shipyards, and he played his hockey in the Pictou County League, also known as the Pictou Town Hockey League. He was playing with his buddies for fun. No disrespect to those who plied their trade in the Town League, but it was basically a high-functioning beer league. Again, I say this because I know: my father, Dan Reid, played for the Hindi Flyers and they liked their postgame pops. Don't believe me? Check out some wisdom from the Pictou *Advocate* published in spring 1982, which gives you a glimpse into just how much the players liked their refreshments: "Close to 200 hockey players, their wives and guests, attended Saturday night's Awards Dinner, with Ernie Knowles preparing a hearty feast at the Pictou Armouries. Bartender Dennis Battist admits, 'We don't run out of drinks often, but tonight, even the ice cubes were liquidated.'" Wayne left that banquet with a ton of hardware. He won awards for the league's Top Scorer, Most Valuable Player, Top Rookie, and All-Star.

The next season is the one that the old-timers around town still talk about. While T-Pot and the Mariners were thrilling hundreds every Saturday night at Hector Arena, the guys in the town league played in front of relatively empty stands during the rest of the week. That didn't seem to bother Woody. He was the offensive juggernaut of a line legendary in Town League status: Woodacre on the right wing, along with Robert Blair at centre and Jackie Martin on the left. They finished 1-2-3 in league scoring with Woody leading the way, with 85 goals and 154 points.

T-Pot had mentioned he always thought Wayne should play in the NHL, and he ultimately did get a chance. This may sound like a hockey fairy tale, but it really happened. In Pictou in 1983 you'd never run across a bigger Montreal Canadiens fan than Donnie Clarke. Donnie would make the trek to Montreal a few times a year to check out his team. He'd always buy the same tickets, always from the same scalper, and he'd sit in the same seats. (Donnie's son David, a good buddy of mine, still follows in his father's footsteps to Montreal. That same scalper calls him "Junior.")

Late in the winter of 1983, when Wayne was wrapping up his season in Pictou, Donnie made one of his usual trips to Montreal. It just so happened that Donnie and his wife, Leona, made this trip with their friends who lived across the street—Dan and Marie Reid, my parents. During this trip the group met up with my folks' good friend Wayne Mundey, a former WHA referee who would go on to a scouting career in the NHL. Donnie was more than excited to tell Wayne, a close friend of Hartford Whalers general manager Larry Pleau, all about this guy from Nova Scotia named Wayne Woodacre. Here was a player, Donnie said, who could score almost at will. He was a late bloomer who never got his shot. Donnie knew Wayne well from the rinks and he was also his boss at the Pictou Shipyard. The press was on, it seemed, to get Wayne Woodacre, the top scorer in the Pictou Town Hockey League, an NHL tryout.

Donnie eventually told Pleau, the Whalers GM, all about this scoring machine from a small fishing town in Nova Scotia. Donnie, who passed away a few years ago, was never shy to strike up a conversation with anyone in the hockey world. "He told Larry, 'You guys need more scoring,'" says longtime Pictou hockey fan Clary Melanson, who has played, coached, and refereed the game for most of his life. "Donnie said, 'I got a young fella in Nova Scotia that can score goals. He can score at random.'"

Trust me, NHL general managers have conversations like this with hockey fans all the time. Small-town hockey aficionados always seem to think that they know a guy who could play in the NHL. But Donnie Clarke didn't give up. On March 1, 1983, he wrote a letter to Pleau, copying Mundey. The letter read, in part:

"You are no doubt wondering why Wayne [Woodacre] has come to no one's attention from a professional point of view.

"Quite candidly, even though he was an excellent player in his junior days, his extracurricular activities were such that his attention to hockey was not always 100%; and his head was going in many different ways at once as is common in many young, rather immature teenagers.

"However, over the last two years Wayne has become married, has a young son, has become very settled and if anything has matured as a hockey player as well as an individual."

Somehow the letter worked. Woodacre was invited to the 1983 Hartford Whalers training camp. The Whalers gave him a workout program for the summer. Soon enough, the day came. One Saturday morning in September 1983, Wayne hopped in a car with Donnie Clarke and Clary Melanson and headed for Hartford, Connecticut. That first day they made it all the way to Boston, where they stayed at a friend of Donnie's for the night. The next day Woodacre, a Pictou Shipyard employee and former Junior B hockey star, arrived in Hartford to try to crack an NHL roster: "Wayne was a shy kid," says Clary. "The first meeting they had the assistant coach got up and he said, 'Okay, this is what's going to happen this week. By the way, if you're late for breakfast it's a fifty-dollar fine. If you're late for practice, it's three hundred.' So, Wayne came out in the lobby, and he said to Donnie and me, 'I'm not going to have a goddamn cent by the time I get home.' I said, 'What do you mean?' He said, 'You get fined for everything.' I said, 'Bud—this is the Show!'"

Soon enough, Donnie bumped into Larry Pleau, who told Donnie and Clary to stick around. The Whalers got them the team rate at the hotel right beside the arena. It appeared that

Woodacre's two-man entourage were going to hunker down at a busy NHL camp. Four teams of twenty players tried out for the Whalers. The September 11, 1983, edition of the *Hartford Courant* listed the names of the eighty players invited to camp and the name of the team that they each played for the season before. The list featured future scoring star and NHL commentator Ray Ferraro and future Hall of Famer Ron Francis. The contributing teams were among the best Junior and minor pro league teams from across the continent: the Sault Ste. Marie Greyhounds, the Peterborough Petes, and the Portland Winterhawks.

Then there was Wayne Woodacre. His team was listed as "Pictou County Intermediate League." The name above Wayne's on the roster was Doug Sulliman, who had scored 22 goals the previous year for the Whalers. "As soon as we arrived there, about two hours after we got to the hotel, Sulliman came knocking on Wayne's door. Doug was from Glace Bay. He was just so glad to see somebody from Nova Scotia," Clary recalls. "Doug was one of those guys . . . you just fell in love with him as soon as you started talking to him. He said, 'If there is anything I can do for you, Wayne, just let me know. Don't feel shy. If you need anything, sticks or anything, just ask the trainers.'" Wayne got what he needed and hit the ice, participating in practices in the morning and intrasquad games at night. It was an eye-opener and a challenge.

For Donnie and Clary, it was the thrill of a lifetime. They sat in for both the practices and the games. "Me and Donnie, we probably enjoyed the trip more than Wayne. We had a few pops. We had some good meals, had a few laughs," says Clary. They sat close to the brass and one time even sat right beside a certain guy who had wrapped up his NHL career with the Whalers a few seasons earlier.

"We were sitting with Gordie Howe on the second day, watching Wayne. The guys were coming out for a practice and Wayne was wearing a white jersey that day. Gordie looked at Donnie, he looked at me, and he said, 'You guys are from Nova Scotia?' We said, 'Yeah.' Gordie said, 'It's not hard to pick out these guys who come off the ponds from up that far.' He looked out onto the ice. That day Wayne was wearing number twelve, and Gordie said, 'Number twelve? Is that the guy you took here?' Right off the bat, Gordie knew. I said to Donnie, 'How did he know that?' Donnie said, 'He knows how guys skate.' It was crazy." Clary chuckles as he tells me this; you can tell this story has stuck with him over the years.

As for Wayne, he was in a world that could not be any further from the not-bright lights of the Pictou Town Hockey League. His roommate was a big defenceman who had been cut from the Olympic team. He was skating with NHLers—future stars. And he was holding his own: "I think he had three or four goals in the intrasquad games," says Clary.

After seven days in Hartford, Donnie and Clary said goodbye to Wayne and drove back to Nova Scotia, leaving the kid behind to chase his dreams. A kid who, in the hockey world, came out of nowhere. It seemed too good to be true.

And then it was over. Wayne got through three rounds of cuts, over two weeks. On the final report before he was sent home, the scouts told Wayne he was a natural goal scorer, no question about that. "They told him that his biggest downfall was his skating, and we kind of knew that going in. These guys, when they came into training camp, they were all built for speed. He was in tough. But he showed really well. We were very proud of him," says Clary.

"It was a great opportunity [for Wayne]. There's no question about that. It only happens once in a lifetime. When Wayne left Hartford, Christ, they gave him about a thousand sticks. They paid his taxi fare from Halifax to Pictou. They paid his airfare, the whole nine yards. He was treated like gold," he adds.

The Whalers sent Wayne home with the promise that they would keep an eye on him. Wayne went back to work at the shipyards and did what he always did in the winter—he played hockey. He kept scoring. "Wayne Gretzky, Eat Your Heart Out," read the caption in a local paper in spring 1984, with a picture of Woodacre scoring his 100th goal of the season that year in the Pictou Town Hockey League.

"Donnie and me, we talked about it after six months or a year later," says Clary. "We bumped into each other, and we said, 'What do you think? Do you think Wayne might try again?' Because he did have kind of an open invitation. He could've called the scouting guys and said, 'I'd really like another shot at it.' But that never came about."

Wayne settled into his life in Pictou. He played hockey, fastball, and golf with the same guys he played with before he tried out for the Hartford Whalers. As the years went by, the story of Wayne Woodacre trying out for the Whalers became folklore around the little town: "We were an old married couple at age twenty-three, twenty-four," says Ruth, of that long-ago Hartford adventure. "Wayne was working at the shipyard. We were set in our ways and partying. He was a small-town boy chasing after the big city, and he wasn't prepared for it. By then, it was almost too late. [But] if he had been groomed from a young age . . ." Ruth does not finish her sentence. It's clear what she means. Not everyone makes the NHL, even if that player has meteoric talent.

Year after year, Wayne would lead the Town League in scoring. He and his old linemates, Jackie Martin and Robert Blair, would play intermediate hockey together for the Pictou County Blues. All three would be smiling as though they were playing in the NHL. Wayne would coach as well—not many future NHLers, but at least one future broadcaster and author.

In the summers you could find Woody playing for Caribou in the local fastball league. His third baseman was T-Pot, who would always throw a one-hopper over to Woody for an out. (Like I've said, we kids imitated the way T-Pot threw a ball as well. One-hopper to first all the time.) Woody was a dad, a husband, an athlete, and a coach. He was a constant presence in the sports scene of a little town.

"I enjoyed it all," says Ruth. "Watching him and his teammates. We went all over the province, following these teams everywhere. And then after our boys finished hockey we continued to go to the rink in Pictou and watch the next groups. We watched kids that weren't our own or related to us. We'd go to the Annapolis Valley and get a cabin and spend March break watching hockey. People would go south on March break. I'd joke and say I'm going north—to Sydney for provincials!"

Wayne Woodacre died on February 2, 2013. He was fifty-two years old. Cancer took his life, but it couldn't take away his legacy. Every September, the people of Pictou—once-upon-a-time kids who perhaps Wayne played with or coached, including T-Pot and a lot of guys who wore number 8—get together and play in the Woody's Slice Memorial Golf Tournament. All the money raised goes to Wayne's home away from home: Hector Arena. The tournament is sold out every year and has through the years raised more than $100,000. "Wayne was a pretty popular fella," says

Ruth. "A lot of people looked up to him. He was well-known in the community. Just that number eight on his back—you always knew who number eight was before he ever turned around. He made a big impact on the community."

Today, when you walk into Hector Arena, there is a display honouring Wayne Woodacre. There's another one that honours Joey MacDonald, the goaltender from town who made it all the way to the NHL about thirty years after Wayne gave it a try. Of the impact Wayne made on the area's local kids, Ruth states, "I think players like Wayne who went and didn't make it [to the NHL] maybe let people know that it was at least a possibility.

"I just went for a walk in town tonight," she continues. "I'll start downtown. I might go into the curling rink. I'll walk way over to the east end of town and then to the top and finish up at the rink. I don't even have to go in but sometimes I'll go in and just look at Wayne's picture. I'll just see who's on the ice and have

Wayne Woodacre (far right) during his time at the Hartford Whalers training camp in fall 1983 alongside NHLer Doug Sulliman (far left) and Donnie Clarke.

a look around and then back out the door and away I go, back downtown. It's kind of nice and sometimes . . . I just feel like I'm going up and saying hello to Wayne."

You don't have to make it to the NHL to be a hockey hero.

"I looked up to Wayne ever since I've known him," says T-Pot.

Likewise, T.

Acknowledgments

First and foremost, a thank-you to all the players, their families, friends, and fans who took part in this project. Their admiration for the game and those who played it is what makes hockey so great and something I truly enjoy writing about.

Kevin Hanson from Simon & Schuster Canada and I made a connection from our very first meeting. A book about local legends needs a legend to believe in it to make it happen, so thank you, Kevin, for believing in me and this project.

To my editors Justin Stoller and Randall Perry, thank you for all your suggestions and making the editing process anything but painful. Justin, you are a true pro, and Randall, thank you for understanding all my local Maritime references in the book. And thanks to Tom Pitoniak for the copyediting. The Bruins fan did a wicked awesome job.

Thanks as well to Paul Barker for the cover design and Karen Kathryn Hollinrake for the photo. Love the look and the passion you guys showed and for making me calm my eyebrows down for the photo shoot.

Of course, lining up with Simon & Schuster Canada would not be possible without my literary agent, Brian Wood. Brian, you have believed in me from day one. Thank you for always being a sympathetic ear and for usually being the first person to believe in my quirky ideas. Brian gets to look at my initial drafts and has developed an incredible amount of patience for typos over the years.

So many people made this project possible. People who never made it into the pages of this book. They may have suggested an idea, helped me track down a number or email address, or helped in any other variety of ways. Big thanks to Darren Colbourne, Adam Binkley, Doug "LEGEND" MacLean, John Shannon, Billy McGuigan, Mike and the Drifters, Troy Shanks, Paul Murray, Mario Therrien, Mike Sim, Brad Murphy, Brent Gretzky, Terry and Pat McTeer, Brad Salamandyk, Cleo, Colby Armstrong, Paul Bromby, Evanka Osmak, Ryan Moynes, The Pictou Mariners, Robbie Marks, Mark Harroun, and David Clarke for always going to the Mariners games with me, David Dort, Craig Clarke, Gair Maxwell, Ruth Woodacre, Aunt Gail, the New Brunswick Sports Hall of Fame, Sean "The Sheriff" McMorrow, Paul Peller, and Jim Nicholson and his book *On the Ice in Pictou.*

And thank you, Internet! Sites like hockeydb.com, elitepros pects.com, hockey-reference.com, and newspapers.com are the best. Local libraries from across the country were a huge help as well.

My mother and father have always been very supportive and have never hesitated to promote my writing. They are both great storytellers and I'd like to think some of that has rubbed off on me. Thanks to my brother, Peter, and sister, Katie, who are always willing to listen and give some needed advice. My family has always shared the love of the game with me throughout my entire life.

To my boys, Cobs and Lou, thank you for always making me

smile and for understanding that sometimes I have work to do. It is work that I truly enjoy and I hope that you will enjoy it one day as well. I hope my love of writing will inspire you to read endlessly throughout your lives. Seeing either of you reading with your night-light on always brings a smile to my face.

Thank you, Mrs. Reid, for always believing in me. Your support seems, much like my annoyance of you, endless. Thanks for understanding my strange obsession with the people that make the game of hockey tick at all levels. And thank you for understanding my obsession with you.